WHALE ADVENTURE

'Sorry, kid,' said third mate Brown. 'Your brother dived to help a chum who had just been pulled down by a shark. That's the last we saw of either of them.'

'But you don't really know that he died,' Roger insisted.

'Look, kid,' Brown explained patiently, 'when a man goes down and doesn't come up, there's only one answer. The boats that came in to pick us up – they rowed all over the place to make sure they weren't missing anybody. No use fooling yourself. The sharks got him. We looked everywhere. You can trust us. We know our business.'

'But you don't know my brother. He's met sharks before and he didn't let them take him. I'll bet he's alive. Couldn't we go out and look again?'

'It ain't no use,' said Brown.

By the same author

AMAZON ADVENTURE
SOUTH SEA ADVENTURE
UNDERWATER ADVENTURE
VOLCANO ADVENTURE
AFRICAN ADVENTURE
ELEPHANT ADVENTURE
SAFARI ADVENTURE
LION ADVENTURE
GORILLA ADVENTURE
DIVING ADVENTURE
CANNIBAL ADVENTURE
TIGER ADVENTURE
ARCTIC ADVENTURE

WHALE ADVENTURE

by

WILLARD PRICE

Illustrated by

PAT MARRIOTT

A Red Fox Book
Published by Random House Children's Books
61–63 Uxbridge Road, London W5 5SA

A division of Random House UK Ltd
London Melbourne Sydney Auckland
Johannesburg and agencies throughout the world

First published in 1960 by Jonathan Cape Ltd
Paperback edition 1973 Knight Books

Red Fox edition 1993

11

Text © Willard Price 1960
Illustrations © Jonathan Cape Ltd 1960

Set in 11/12.5pt Baskerville by Intype, London
Printed and bound in Great Britain by
CPI Antony Rowe, Chippenham, Wiltshire

Addresses for companies within The Random House Group Limited
can be found at:
www.randomhouse.co.uk/offices.htm

RANDOM HOUSE UK Limited Reg. No. 954009
www.kidsatrandomhouse.co.uk

Papers used by Random House UK Limited
are natural, recyclable products made from wood grown in
sustainable forests. The manufacturing processes conform to
the environmental regulations of the country of origin.

ISBN 9780099184713

Contents

1	The Bird with Twenty Wings	11
2	Two 'Gents' on a Whaler	19
3	Captain Grindle Amuses Himself	26
4	The First Whale	40
5	Nantucket Sleigh Ride	45
6	Man Overboard	51
7	A Quarter of a Mile Down	57
8	The Wolves of the Sea	62
9	Fighting Killer Whales	70
10	Cat-O'-Nine-Tails	78
11	The Great Bull	87
12	The Giant Nutcracker	91
13	Wild Ride	99
14	Alone	105
15	How to Steer a Whale	109
16	Rescue	116
17	The Ghost in the Fog	124
18	Grindle Takes a Blubber Bath	132
19	Grindle Shakes Hands	138
20	The Mako Shark	143
21	Mutiny	150
22	Escape – Almost	156
23	Can a Whale Sink a Ship?	166

24	The Wreck of the *Killer*	173
25	Adrift	185
26	An Albatross Named Bill	190
27	Winged Messenger	196
28	Whaling the Easy Way	204
29	Marvels of the Factory Ship	208
30	To African Adventure	218

To the
YOUNG PRICES
of Holden

WHALE ADVENTURE

1
The Bird with Twenty Wings

On all the hills of Honolulu people looked to the sea. Spectators crowded the docks lining the harbour.

They were all gazing in the same direction. They paid no attention to the steamers and yachts, cargo vessels and tugs. They did not bother to glance at the helicopter passing overhead, or the plane setting out for San Francisco.

These they could see any day.

They looked at something that seemed to have come from another world. It was the kind of ship that used to take men sailing and whaling a century ago.

It had no funnels, no black smoke, no grinding, growling machinery. Its three masts towered more than a hundred feet high. From them hung its twenty great sails, drying in the still, sunny air. It looked like a huge bird about to fly away.

'A fine sight!' said someone.

'Didn't think there were any of those old beauties left,' said another.

'Beauty my eye,' said a man who looked like a sailor. 'You wouldn't think she was such a beauty if you knew what happens to the men who sail on her.'

'Hope it isn't too bad,' said a new voice, 'because *we're* going to sail on her.'

'I'm sorry for you,' said the sailor, and looked up at the newcomer. He saw Hal Hunt, tall, well built, nineteen years old, his deeply tanned face lit by a pleasant smile.

'Well,' admitted the sailor, 'you look as if you could take care of yourself. But I hope this kid isn't going too.'

Roger bristled up and tried to look as big and tough as his thirteen years would permit. He was about to make a smart reply when Mr Scott cut in.

'I don't think we'll have any trouble,' he said as he and the two boys pressed on through the crowd.

The sailor shook his head doubtfully. But Hal and Roger felt confidence in their older companion. Everything would be all right so long as they were accompanied by the scientist, Arthur Scott of the American Museum.

Still, the sailor's remarks left them a bit uneasy.

Reaching the edge of the dock they climbed down a ladder into a waiting launch and were taken out towards the great bird with the twenty white wings. The closer they came the more uneasy they grew. For the ship itself was not white and beautiful like its sails. It was a black evil-looking hulk, and from it drifted the strong smell of whale oil and rancid blubber.

Now the name of the bark could be seen on the stern and it was not a pretty name. *Killer* was the name, and the home port was St Helena.

'She's named after the killer-whale,' said Mr Scott. 'That's the most vicious and deadly of all the whales.'

'Where is St Helena?' asked Roger.

'It's an island far down in the South Atlantic. It has always been a great whaling port. Only fifty years ago you could see as many as a hundred whaling ships in the harbour at one time. And there were hundreds more in northern ports.'

'Only fifty years?' said Hal. 'I thought it was centuries ago.'

'No — whaling under sail was not as ancient as you might suppose. As late as 1907 New Bedford had a fleet of twenty-two whalers. Of course, today the business has been taken over by the big factory ships — but with the new demand for whale products a few of the old sailing vessels have been put back into service. That gives us a chance to see how whaling used to be done. And that's why the American Museum wants me to make a complete record of the operations and take motion pictures for the museum's library.'

'Has the captain really agreed to take you?'

'Yes. But he says he won't sail until he can get two more men. Two of his crew deserted — he has to fill their places.'

'And that's where we come in,' said Hal.

'Exactly. You've never sailed in a square-rigger, but he probably wouldn't be able to find anybody who has. You know something about the sea, after sailing your own boat all over the Pacific.[1] Even Roger is not too young to be useful as a mess-boy or look-out — there are dozens of jobs he could do on a sailing ship.'

He glanced up at the savage black hulk of the *Killer*.

'The only question is — do you want to go? I'm not going to press you, and I don't want any quick answer. It's up to you. I can tell you it's hard work — so hard that crews accustomed to the soft duties on a steamer won't touch it. I can tell you, too, that

[1] For the previous adventures of Hal and Roger Hunt, see the books *Amazon Adventure*, *South Sea Adventure*, *Underwater Adventure*, and *Volcano Adventure*, by Willard Price.

14

the captain looks to me like a bully and a brute. That's another reason he has trouble finding men. I'm glad you cabled your father and got his consent, because I can't be responsible for you. You're on your own. After you've seen the captain and looked over the ship you will still have time to back out if you want to.'

The launch hugged in under the black counter of the *Killer*. Looking up from this point the sight was dizzying. Up they looked to the gunwale over which a rope ladder dangled. Up to the bottom of a lifeboat swinging from its davits. On up the three masts, the mainmast and foremast, square-rigged, the mizenmast carrying fore-and-aft sails in the manner of a bark. Up past mainsail and foresail, topsails and topgallant sails, royals and trysails, up to the look-out's cage at the very tip of the mainmast a good hundred and ten feet above water.

Loving the sea as they did, they had many times studied pictures and descriptions of the old square-riggers, but this was the first time they had seen one. It gave them stomach-butterflies to think of climbing those ratlines that went skyward like narrow spider-webs, up, up to where the gently swaying masthead seemed to scrape the clouds. If it made them dizzy to look up, how would they feel looking *down* from that unsteady basket, say in a storm, when the sway of the mast would be anything but gentle?

'Oh, a sailor's life is a jolly life,' sang Roger, but he was quite out of tune and didn't sound very convincing.

'All right, over you go,' said Scott.

15

The boys came out of their trance and scrambled up the rope ladder, Scott following. They tumbled over the rail on to the deck.

Was the ship on fire? Red flames shot up and white steam filled the air. Men seemed to be fighting the fire. The boys came closer. Now they could see that the fire was confined inside a brick wall. Huge black pots, each big enough to hold several men, rested in the flames. Men hauled great chunks of meat as big as themselves across the deck and dumped them into the pots.

'Just trying-out,' said Mr Scott. 'That's blubber. Blubber is the whale's overcoat. It's very fat. They put the blubber into the pots and cook the oil out of it. It's called trying-out.'

The men, in ragged blood-and-oil-stained clothes and unshaved beards looked as rough as pirates. The roughest and biggest of them gave orders. He noticed the newcomers and walked growling towards them as if prepared to throw them bodily off his ship. His eyes were large and bulging, like big marbles; his mouth had a mean twist to starboard; and his chin, covered with black bristles like porcupine quills, projected forward like the prow of a pirate ship.

'What do you want — ' he began gruffly, then recognized Mr Scott. 'Oh, you're the scientific fellow.' He made an obvious effort to be more polite. 'Welcome aboard. Are you ready to pay me for your passage?'

'I am,' said Mr Scott, producing from his breast pocket a large roll of notes. 'I believe that's the price you asked for three weeks' passage.'

'All that,' exclaimed Hal, 'for passage on this?'
At once he realized he should not have said it. After
all, it was none of his business.

The captain glared. 'Who's this smart alec? What
does he know about the cost of running a ship?
And how about all the trouble I'm going to have
with the science fellow stumbling around in our
way?' He stuffed the money into his trouser pocket
and advanced upon Hal. 'By the Holy Harry, I wish
I had you in my crew. I'd trim you down to size!'

Hal did not flinch. He was as tall as the captain,
not so heavily built but perhaps just as wiry and
strong.

'Start trimming,' he said with a smile, 'because I
think I'm going to be in your crew.'

Mr Scott hastened to pour oil on troubled waters.

'It's my fault,' he said. 'I should have begun with
introductions. Captain Grindle, this is Hal Hunt

and his brother Roger. You are short of two men — perhaps they will sign on. They've had some sea experience. Of course, they don't know much about square-riggers.'

'Nobody does,' growled the captain.

'But they will learn as fast as anyone you could pick up. They're used to roughing it. Their father is a famous collector of animals for zoos and circuses. He has sent his boys on various trips to collect wild animals, and on scientific expeditions to teach them something about the world we live in. They'd learn a lot on your ship.'

'They would that,' agreed the captain sourly. 'I'd learn them things they'd never forget. But I don't know about taking on a couple of gents.'

He spat out the word 'gents'.

'They'll want special favours,' he went on. 'Believe me, they won't get them. They'll sleep in the fo'c'sle with the rest of the crew. They'll eat what's put before 'em. They'll step lively or smart for it, and I don't care if their father is the King of Siam.'

'Don't worry,' said Hal. 'Our father isn't the King of Siam. And we're not "gents". We want no favours.'

'Like as not too soft for this kind of work,' grumbled the captain. 'Let me see your hands.'

The four palms held out for his inspection were hard and tough. The captain may have been surprised but he wouldn't admit it.

'Soft as butter,' he said scornfully. 'You'll have blisters as big as plums before you're on this ship a day. Oh well, if I can't get what I want I have to take what I can get. Come down and sign on.'

2
Two 'Gents' on a Whaler

Captain Grindle clumped down the steps to his cabin. Hal and Roger, about to follow, were stopped by Mr Scott.

'I like this fellow less and less,' said Scott in a low voice. 'I've got to go with him — but you don't have to. I'm sorry I got you into this. Why don't you just back out now before it's too late?'

Hal looked at Roger. He felt he could take what was coming, but it would be harder on his young brother.

'It's up to the boy,' Hal said.

Roger, whose heart had sunk into his shoes at the thought that they might after all miss this great adventure of sails and whales, was suddenly happy again.

'If it's up to me,' he said, 'let's go,' and he led the way down the steps.

On a table in the captain's cabin lay the papers. Hal began to look them over.

'Come, come,' said Captain Grindle impatiently. 'Do you think I have time to stand around while you read all the small print? Sign and have done with it. I'm paying you a one-three-hundredth lay.'

Hal knew the system of lays. Whalers got no wages. Each got a share of the profits of the voyage. This share was called a lay. Hal's lay of one three-hundredth meant that if the ship came back with three hundred gallons of whale oil Hal would be paid the price of one gallon. It was a very small lay.

'And my brother?' asked Hal.

The captain's eyes flashed. 'You don't expect me to pay a child! He goes as an apprentice. He gets nothing but his food and bunk — and won't be worth that.'

It didn't seem fair to Roger. But he held his tongue. After all, he was taking this trip for experience, not money. What bothered him most was being called a child. Wasn't he thirteen years old and so big that some people took him for fifteen or sixteen? He itched for a chance to show this contemptuous captain that he was no child.

When the papers were signed the captain showed Mr Scott his cabin, a small room next to his own. 'Really the first mate's,' he said. 'But since I've got no first for this trip, you may have it.'

He turned to the boys. 'Go up and ask for Mr Durkins. Second mate. He'll tell you the difference between a clove hitch and a donkey's breakfast. And mind you learn fast. You'll be no use to me on a three weeks cruise if it takes you three weeks to learn which end your head is screwed on. Get your gear aboard this afternoon. We sail before dawn.'

'Thank you,' said Hal, going out of the door.

'Wait a minute, young fella,' bawled the captain.

'The first thing you want to learn is to say "sir" when you speak to an officer.'

'Thank you, sir,' said Hal, and went on deck followed by Roger.

They found Mr Durkins waiting for them. He was as rough as gravel but he had a ready smile.

'I usually get the job of showing the greenies the ropes,' he said. 'First you might like to see where you bunk.'

He led the way forward and down the hatch into the fo'c'sle.

It was dark. There were no portholes. The only light came from two sputtering whale-oil lamps. They also sent out black smoke and nauseating fumes.

There were other smells, walls of them, waves of them, smells so strong that they seemed like something solid that could only be cut through with a hatchet or a knife. Clothes hanging from pegs stank of dead whales. There was no ventilation except through the half-opened hatch. That would be closed in rough weather. There was a smell of mouldy rags and mildewed boots and unwashed bodies and decayed food. And the heat made all the smells more suffocating.

'Here's where you doss down,' said the mate, indicating two bunks, one above the other.

Hal examined the bunks. The thin pad lay on wooden boards. There were no springs, no bedding, no pillow.

'How about blankets?' Hal asked.

'Blankets! Man alive, this is the tropics. You're lucky to get a donkey's breakfast.'

Roger remembered the captain had said something about a donkey's breakfast.

'What's a donkey's breakfast?' he asked.

'This pad.'

'Why do they call it a donkey's breakfast?'

'I don't know. Because it's stuffed with straw, I guess.'

'A pretty slim breakfast,' said Hal, pinching the edge of the pad. It was not quite an inch thick. The boards would feel pretty hard through it.

'Good for your back,' laughed the mate. 'Why, they tell me the best people sleep on boards these days. The doctors are all for it. 'Course, nothin' but the best would satisfy Cap Grindle.' He laughed again. 'The best boards, the best brig and the best cat.'

The brig, Hal knew, was the jail, and the cat must be the cat-o'-nine-tails or whip used to flog unruly sailors.

'You're joking about the cat,' Hal said. 'I suppose that isn't used any more. The law doesn't allow it.'

This struck the mate as very funny.

'The law,' he said, between gasps of laughter. 'The law, you say! Believe you me, the captain makes his own law on this ship.' He stopped laughing and his face suddenly took on a look of savage ferocity. In an instant he was changed from a carefree sailor into a snarling animal. He glanced up at the open hatch, then lowered his voice to a harsh whisper.

'You may as well know about it now,' he said. 'You'll learn soon enough. Why does ol' man Grindle have trouble getting men? Why did those two desert? Why is he willing to take on greenies like you? Because he needs new feed for his cat, that's why. Scarce a man on board who hasn't felt it. Even the first mate — that's why he quit. See here.'

He switched off his shirt. His back was ribbed with purple welts standing up a quarter of an inch high. At points the skin was still broken and festering.

'But why do you stand it?' asked Hal. 'You could report it to the Honolulu police. Why don't you all desert?'

'Listen, chum, you don't understand. We been out a year already from St Helena. We get no wages — just a lay — and that isn't paid till we get home. Them as desert now lose everything they've earned. D'ye wonder a man thinks twice before he deserts? No, there are only two things we can do. One is to be patient-like till we get home.'

Hal waited for him to go on. When he did not, Hal prompted:

'And what's the other thing you can do?'

Durkins cast a look round at the empty bunks. 'Walls have ears,' he said. 'And you have ears, and how do I know I can trust 'em? What's the other thing we can do? Use your imagination. No harm in that — but remember I didn't say anything.'

Mutiny. The word stood out as plainly as if he had shouted it at the top of his lungs. Not for nothing had the boys read innumerable stories of mutiny on the high seas. Here conditions were prime for mutiny. The captain, without a first officer to back him up, stood alone against a disgruntled crew. If he were put out of the way they might sail the ship to some smugglers' lair, sell the whale oil and the ship itself and divide the proceeds.

But could such a thing happen in this day and age? The boys knew it could happen and did happen. Even during their own brief voyaging of the Pacific, from San Francisco to Japan and back through the South Seas, several mutinies had been reported.

The Pacific, they knew, is a still unconquered ocean. It is bigger than the whole land surface of the globe. It is sprinkled with more than twenty-five thousand islands, half of them uninhabited.

It is the paradise of both honest men and rascals. So much of it is so far from police stations and law-courts that men do as they please or as they must. And men who choose to disappear may hide in its vast distances more effectively than in the thickest jungles of Africa.

Hal reflected that this voyage might turn out to be even more of an adventure than he had expected.

'Now I'll show you topside,' said the mate, and they climbed to the deck. The clean fresh air seemed like a tonic after the hot stink of the fo'c'sle.

'You've got to know the names of things,' said the mate, 'so when you're told to man the down-haul you won't lay hold of a halyard, and all like that. Now then, you know the three masts — the foremost, mainmast and mizenmast. The horizontal spars the sails hang from are the yards. When you roll up the sails that's reefing 'em, and you tie them tight with those little strings called gaskets — '

He went on to point out and describe all the complicated gear of the most complicated of sailing ships — lifts, clews, bunts, braces, tacks, sheets, shrouds, ratlines, rings, crosstrees, foot-ropes, buoy-ropes, wheel-ropes, belaying pins, catheads, fore-stays, backstays, booms, sprits, davits, and so on and on, concluding with twenty different sails, each with its own particular name.

As he talked he kept glancing at them with a sly grin. He was having a good time at their expense. He thought they didn't know what he was talking about. Finally he said:

'There, I'll bet you can't remember half of what I've told you. What's that sail?'

'Spanker.' The boys spoke together.

'And that one?'

'Gaff-topsyl.'

'What's the difference between a martingale boom and a whisker boom?'

He got the right answer.

He went on with a complete cross-examination. The boys made some mistakes, but thanks to their keen interest in sailing, their schooner experience and much reading, their percentage of error was small.

'Not bad,' Durkins had to admit. Then, as if fearing that the boys might be too pleased with themselves, he went on:

'But it's one thing to name 'em and another thing to use 'em. Wait till you try reefing sails in a storm a hundred feet above deck — or rowing one of those little boats out and tackling a whale that can smash your craft to smithereens with one flick of his tail. Then you'll find out what it takes to be a whaler.'

3
Captain Grindle Amuses Himself

Roger floated above the clouds.

They seemed like clouds, the twenty white sails that billowed beneath him.

He was in the 'rings', a sort of basket or crow's-nest at the top of the mainmast. A hundred feet down was the deck of the *Killer,* but he could not see it. He could see nothing below him but the white clouds of canvas. For a while he was alone, soaring through the sky like a bird or a plane, white clouds below him and more white clouds, real ones, above.

Not quite alone. One man shared his heaven. In the rings at the head of the foremast stood Jiggs, one of the crew. He, too, could not see the ship beneath. But he was not there to look at the ship. Both he and Roger were posted as look-outs to watch for whales.

There they stood, only thirty feet apart, but with an impassable canyon between them. It was as if they were each perched on a mountain-top separated by a deep valley filled with cloud. The cloud ended only a few feet below them and it was easy to imagine that you could walk across this white floor from the head of the mainmast to the head of the foremast. But when you remembered that the floor was not reliable and would treacherously let you plunge to your death on the deck a hundred feet below, it made your head swim and hands grip the rail of your dizzy basket.

Of course, it was the basket that was dizzy — Roger wouldn't admit that he was. The basket was going around in circles. The sea was fairly smooth, but there was enough of a swell to roll the ship slightly from side to side and make it lazily heave and pitch.

Those on deck might not notice the motion, but a movement of a few inches there was exaggerated to many feet at the masthead. So it was that Roger was spun round and round until he began to have a distinctly uncomfortable feeling in the pit of his stomach.

This was his first day of whaling. The *Killer* had left Honolulu at dawn. After their interview with Captain Grindle the boys and Mr Scott had gone ashore for their gear. There Scott had said goodbye to his colleague, Sinclair, who had been unable to go with him on the *Killer* because the captain had insisted that one 'science fellow' was enough to bother with. Hal and Roger had said their own goodbyes to their friends on the schooner *Lively Lady*, on which they had sailed the far Pacific. The schooner was still under charter by the American Museum, and the skipper, Captain Ike, and the

Polynesian man, Omo, would look after it until the return of the *Killer* in three weeks.

The first night on board had not been too happy. The first surprise came at dinner-time.

There was no dining-saloon for the crew, not even a table. The men formed in line and walked past a small window in the wall of the galley (kitchen). Through this window the cook thrust out to each man a pan of meat and beans and a chunk of hard-tack (ship-biscuit).

Then you could look for a place to sit down. Of course, there were no chairs. You might sit on the fo'c'sle head, or on a hatch cover, or on the deck itself.

Or you could eat standing up. This was not too bad because the eating did not take long. It was not the sort of food you would linger over. You got it down as fast as possible. In five minutes it was stowed away.

As for the hard-tack, it was well named. It was so hard that the best teeth could scarcely make a dent in it, and most of the men threw their biscuits overside or tried to hit the gulls and terns that wheeled above the ship.

Having emptied their pans the boys were about to take them back to the galley when a sailor prompted:

'Clean 'em first.'

'Where's the water?' Hal asked.

'Water my hat!' exclaimed the sailor. 'What do you think this is, a bloomin' yacht? You'll be lucky if you get enough water to drink — there's none to spare for washin'.'

28

He pulled some rope-yarn from his pocket. It was a tangled mass almost as fluffy as absorbent cotton. He wiped his pan, then threw the sticky wad into the sea. He gave some of the yarn to the boys and they followed the same procedure. Then they returned their pans at the galley window.

'You'll soon get the hang of it,' said the sailor who had supplied them with the rope-yarn. 'My name's Jimson. Any time you get stuck, perhaps I can help out.'

'Thanks a lot,' said Hal, and introduced himself and his brother. 'But I don't understand it. Here we are still in harbour — there surely ought to be plenty of fresh water on board.'

'And so there is,' agreed Jimson. 'But you never know when you leave port on one of these sailing tubs how long it will be before you make port again. You're pretty much at the mercy of wind and weather. 'Course, you could fill up the hold with tanks of water, but then what would you do for space to store your whale oil? And, believe me, the skipper puts whale oil before water. Whale oil means money, water only means lives. If it came right down to it, I'm sure he'd rather have a few of us go raving mad o' thirst than crawl back into port with a light load o'oil.'

'But you must use water to wash your clothes,' Hal said.

'We do — but not fresh water. Come back and I'll show you. There's our clothes-line.' He pointed to a coil of rope beside a barrel. 'Once we get moving we'll soak our dirty clothes in that barrel — it contains a weak acid solution — then we'll tie them to the end of that line and throw it overboard. We'll drag that bundle of clothes through the sea for two or three days, and when we haul it out I'll bet the clothes will be as clean as if you had put them through one of those newfangled washing-machines. Of course, there may be a few holes in them where the sharks have closed their jaws on them.'

'Do the sharks ever tear them off that line?'

'No. One taste, and they let them go. That's what usually happens. But a couple o'months ago one fool of a shark swallowed the whole bundle. Probably there was some blood on the cloth that made him think it was edible. That shark must have been real surprised when he found he couldn't get away. He was towed behind the ship nobody knows how long until someone noticed him floundering about and hauled him in. We opened him up and there were our clothes. They had to be dragged another three days to get the shark-smell out of them.'

The boys did very little sleeping that night. They could not make their bones comfortable on the hard boards of their bunks, and they were excited by their new surroundings and the trip before them.

There were about twenty other men in the room, some trying to sleep, others sitting on the edges of their bunks talking and smoking. The smoke from their cigarettes and pipes, the fumes from the whale-oil lamps, the smell of blood and blubber and bilge-water — all this plus the heat made breathing difficult. The boys were not sorry when at four in the morning the second mate bellowed down through the hatch:

'All hands on deck!'

In the grey light of dawn the *Killer* sailed from Honolulu. On the right lay Pearl Harbor, scene of death and destruction when Japan entered the Second World War. As if to balance this place of terrible memory, on the left was one of the loveliest and happiest spots in the world — the long curve of Waikiki Beach and bold Diamond Head wearing the pink halo of approaching sunrise.

Roger, standing by the rail enjoying the view, was roused by a kick in the rear that almost lifted him from the deck. He turned, fighting mad, clenching his fists for battle. The bulging eyes of Captain Grindle glared down at him.

'I'll have nobody loafing on this ship,' growled the captain.

'Sorry, sir, I was just waiting for orders.'

'You'll get your orders in the seat of your pants if you don't step lively.'

He looked round with a sly grin.

'I'll find you something to do.' He scanned the deck for a job that would be hard enough, something that would tax the strength and courage of a young boy. Finally he glanced up the swaying mast.

Roger hoped he would not be sent aloft. Not just now. Some other time he would like it, but now he felt a little faint for loss of sleep and his breakfast of overripe meat had not agreed with him. The captain seemed to guess the boy's uneasiness.

'That's the place for you,' he laughed savagely.

'Up in the rings, and be quick about it. Jiggs is up the foremast. You shinny up the main. All the way to the peak. And you're not going up there to look at the view. Watch for whales, and if you see a spout sing out. Let's see how sharp your eyes are. If you spot a whale before Jiggs does I'll let you come down. If you don't, you'll stay there until you do, and I don't care if it takes a week. Got no use for babes on deck. Get up there into your cradle, and I hope it rocks you sick.'

Roger was half-way up the ratlines to the first platform before this speech was finished. He had never climbed anything so unsteady as this wobbling rope ladder. He would be glad to reach the solid safety of the first platform, or 'top', as it was called.

He was about to go through the opening in the platform when another bellow came from below.

'Not through the lubber's hole,' roared the captain. 'I'll have no lubbers on this ship. Up around by the futtock shrouds.'

Perhaps he hoped to confuse the boy. But Roger knew that the hole he had been about to pass through was called the lubber's hole. And he knew the futtock shrouds were those iron rods fastened at one end to the mast and at the other to the outer edge of the platform. To climb them he must leave the rope ladder and go up hand over hand with the skill of a monkey, while his feet dangled in space.

Half-way up a lurch of the vessel loosened his grip and he hung suspended by one hand, swinging like a pendulum in a grandfather's clock.

33

A roar of laughter came from below. The captain was thoroughly enjoying himself. Several of the crew had gathered now, but they did not join in the laughter. Hal started up the ratlines to the relief of his brother. A sharp order from the captain stopped him.

Every time the windjammer swayed to starboard Roger was directly over the try-pots in which blubber from the last whale catch was still boiling. If he fell into one of those great steaming vats the comedy would turn to tragedy. But it would still be comedy to the warped mind of Captain Grindle. A wide grin made the porcupine bristles on his chin and cheeks stand out like spears as his eyes passed from the clinging figure to the try-pots and back again. The steam curled up like a snake around the hanging body. Hal edged close to the pots. If the boy fell he might catch him, or at least yank him from the boiling oil in time to save his life.

There came a gasp of relief from the crew and a disappointed grunt from the captain when a list to port swung Roger against the shroud, which he was now able to grip with both hands and his feet as well. He clung there trembling for an instant, then slowly inched his way up over the edge of the top and collapsed on the platform.

A cheer rose from the crew. It was checked at once by the harsh voice of Captain Grindle.

'You varmint! Is this a time to take a nap? I'll wake you up.'

He seized a belaying-pin and flung it upward with

all his great strength. It struck the underside of the top with a resounding whack.

Roger struggled to his feet. He stood swaying dizzily, one arm round the mast.

The crash of the belaying-pin had brought Mr Scott up from his cabin. He turned to Hal.

'What's going on?'

'Just a big bully having some fun,' said Hal bitterly. 'Grindle ordered Roger into the rings. Wouldn't let him go through the lubber's hole. Nothing would have pleased the brute better than to see him drop into the try-pots and get boiled in oil.'

The captain, cursing, grabbed another belaying-pin and hurled it aloft. His aim was good. The heavy wooden club passed through the lubber's hole and struck Roger on the elbow.

Hal and Mr Scott at once began to force their way through the crowd, determined to overpower the captain. The men opened a path to let them through. They were eager to see someone challenge the authority of the master.

The captain saw the two men coming. His eyes shone with evil pleasure and his hand went back to his hip where a revolver rested in its holster.

Then the way was suddenly blocked by the sailor called Jimson. Hal and Scott found themselves held firmly in the grip of the big seaman.

'Stop it, you fools!' said Jimson in a voice just above a rasping whisper. 'You'll get yourselves killed. You'll only make it worse for the kid.' Then he leaned close to Hal's ear, making sure that the captain should not overhear him. 'This ain't the time. The time is coming, but it ain't now.'

Captain Grindle, seeing that he was not to be attacked, roared with laughter.

'What's the matter, gents?' he cried scornfully. 'Why don't you come on? The welcome mat is out. Reception committee is waiting. Step right up, gents — tea will be served.' He spun his revolver around two fingers. 'Pink tea. Will you have lemon or cream? I'll send a cup aloft to your baby brother.'

He fired a shot into the air, not directly at Roger but close enough so that the boy, who was once more climbing the ratlines, heard the whistle of the bullet.

Again Hal and Scott struggled to get at the captain, but several of the crew held them back. Again Jimson whispered harshly: 'This ain't the time. The time is coming, but this ain't it.'

'Cowards and softies!' cried the captain. 'I got nothing but cowards and softies on my ship. The whole pack o' ye wouldn't dare face up to a real man. Now get for'ard and be quick about it.' He fired two shots over their heads. The men retired sullenly towards the fo'c'sle.

Roger, leaving the top behind him, was climbing higher. For the platform called the 'top' is not the top. It is only the head of the lower section of the mast. Two-thirds of the mast rise above it.

Roger thought the mast would never end. He felt like Jack climbing the beanstalk that reached all the way up to another world. He could not use his right arm. The blow from the belaying-pin had not broken any bones, but it had so bruised the elbow that he could not straighten or flex the arm without acute pain.

He tucked the hand within his belt and held to the ratlines with his left hand only. At every rise he must release his grip and transfer his hand to the next higher rung. This might have been easy to do on a wooden ladder, but on a ladder of rope that swung here and there like a loose cobweb at every motion of the ship he was in constant danger of clutching at a rung which was no longer where he had just seen it.

Every near-miss brought a snort of laughter from Captain Grindle, who was now Roger's sole audience. Nothing would so tickle the captain's distorted sense of humour as to see the young 'gent' come to grief.

Roger was determined not to give him that satisfaction. He would not fall, and he would not fail. He was going to reach the rings.

Every time he looked up at them they seemed as far away as ever. It was as if the more he climbed the more an invisible hand drew them a bit higher. At times he must stop and do nothing but cling for his life, as a gust of wind caught his cobweb and whipped it about.

At last he crawled up into the rings, and felt as if he had returned to a solid world when he gripped the iron hoop tightly bolted to the mast. True, the whole basket made dizzy circles in the sky, but it was firm ground compared with the rope ladder.

He looked down at the disappointed master, now almost completely hidden from view by the sails.

Captain Grindle shook his fist as if Roger had deliberately offended him by arriving safely in the rings.

'Remember,' yelled the captain, 'you'll sight first, or stay there till you do.'

Of course, that was not fair. Sighting the spout of a whale is not easy. Experience helps, and Jiggs had had experience, plenty of it.

The beginner is apt to think he sees the spout of a whale when it is only the spume of a breaking wave. Later he gets to know the difference. The spray from a wave-crest is irregular and quickly loses its force. The spout of a whale is like the spurt of water from a high-pressure hose.

And yet it doesn't quite look like water, because it isn't water. Whalers of the nineteenth century supposed it to be water. They supposed the whale to be spitting out water it had taken in by mouth while under the sea.

Now we know that the column of white is steam, not water. The giant of the deeps is letting off steam. The air that he has held in his lungs during his half-hour or more beneath the sea is forcibly expelled. Having been retained so long within the warm body of the whale the air is at the blood temperature of whales and humans, about 98.6 degrees Fahrenheit. It is full of moisture because it has been inside a moist body.

When the whale blows out the warm wet air it condenses to form a mist, just as a man's breath does when exhaled on a frosty morning. So a whale's spout is just a magnificent column of mist rising twenty, thirty, forty feet high. From the rings or crow's-nest of a whaler it can be seen as far as seven miles away.

The spout comes from the whale's nose, located on top of his head. Roger, clutching the rail and looking out to sea, tried to remember some things Mr Scott had told him about whales. Mr Scott had for many years made a scientific study of whales and their habits.

'If you ever have to watch for whales,' he said to Roger, 'keep your eye out for a white palm tree. That's what it looks like, the whale's spout. It goes up in a column and then branches out at the top. And it isn't straight up and down. It leans a little. When you see the spout you can tell which way the whale is going, because the spout always leans forward.'

'Do all whales have the same kind of spout?' Roger had asked.

'No. The palm-tree spout is made by the sperm-whale. His nose has only one nostril, so his tree of steam has only one trunk. If you see two trunks you are probably looking at a rorqual. They have two nostrils and send up twin jets that divide at the top and fall over in two branches like the boughs of a willow. And this twin willow doesn't lean forward, it stands straight up.'

4

The First Whale

Roger now scanned the sea, looking for a white palm with a single trunk, or a willow with two.

He knew he was more likely to see the palm than the willow. The two-nostril whales were best hunted far down in the seas of snow and ice near the South Pole. But the sperm-whale is a tropical animal and loves the warm waters near the Equator.

Whalers of the past hunted it there so relentlessly that it became scarce. Now, after a half-century of rest, sperm-whales were once more fairly plentiful in the warm seas between Hawaii and Tahiti.

And so many new uses have been found for all the parts of this great animal that no richer treasure can be discovered in the sea than a big sperm-whale. So Roger felt a thrill of importance at the thought that the winning of such a treasure might depend upon him.

Of course, Jiggs would probably sight one first. But just now Roger noticed that Jiggs was not looking out to sea. He was looking at Roger. Presently he called across to the boy:

'Cap was a bit rough on ye.'

'Is he always so mean?'

'You haven't seen the half of it yet. My advice to you is, keep your eyes skinned for a whale.'

For an hour, and then for another hour, Roger searched the sea. What a hopeless task it seemed. You couldn't look everywhere at once. While you were staring in one direction a whale might be spouting to high heaven behind you.

He revolved like a radar screen trying to cover the whole circle of the sea every ten seconds. His own revolving, plus the wheeling of his high basket, did not help that uneasy feeling at the pit of his stomach. His eyes became tired and blurred. When he closed them for a moment he could still see nothing but leaping blue waves. His nerves were tight and his arm pained badly.

What was so hard for him seemed to be easy for Jiggs. The sailor had had long practice. A quick glance about him every few seconds was all he needed.

He looked at the boy with sympathy, remembering his own hard experiences as a lad on a whaling ship. He had heard the captain's threat — that if Roger did not sight a whale he would stay there until he did.

They had been watching for three hours when Jiggs, in one of his quick surveys, caught sight of a white jet rising from the sea on the starboard bow.

He was about to sing out when he remembered Roger. The boy did not see the spout. He was looking in exactly the opposite direction, but he was turning and soon would be facing towards the whale.

41

Jiggs still had a chance to make the first call. There was always keen competition between look-outs. Jiggs was not used to letting any look-out beat him, if he could help it. But now, sympathy for the greenhorn held his tongue.

The whale spouted again. It was barely two miles off. Someone on deck might see it. In that case both look-outs would be disgraced, and might even be in for a flogging.

Jiggs could have told Roger where to look. He did not, because he had already seen enough of the boy's courage to know that he would refuse to sing out for a whale if he knew that Jiggs had seen it first. No, the lad must discover it for himself.

Roger was now facing directly forward. Now his eyes turned to starboard. He was looking straight towards the whale, but that beast, hidden in the waves, chose this instant to be contrary and was sending up no spout. Roger's gaze turned farther to starboard. Jiggs gave up his generous plan and opened his mouth to call 'Thar she blows' as the whale sent up another white palm tree.

He never did let out that call. Roger, though not looking directly towards the whale, saw the jet from the corner of his eye.

He had known for years that the look-out sighting a whale is supposed to call 'Thar she blows!' But now he was so excited that he could not think of the words. He jumped up and down and yelled: 'Whale! Whale!'

The captain came running from the afterdeck calling:

'Where away?'

'Over there,' yelled Roger, forgetful that the canvas between him and the deck would prevent the captain from seeing where he was pointing.

'Where, you young fool? Weather or lee?'

Roger tried to collect his wits. 'Four points on the weather-bow, sir. About two miles off.'

'What kind?'

'Sperm-whale.'

Captain Grindle came swarming up the ratlines. When a whale is sighted the captain belongs in the rings. In an amazingly short time Grindle made the masthead and stood beside Roger.

He looked away, four points on the weather-bow, and saw — nothing. He fixed an icy stare upon Roger.

'If you got me up here on a fool's errand — '

'I'm quite sure I saw something, sir.'

But was he sure? He had seen it only out of the corner of his eye. When he had looked straight towards it, it was gone. The breeze had freshened and every once in a while the white crest of a wave would burst into spray. Perhaps this was what he had seen.

The same thought had evidently occurred to the captain. He gazed to starboard for a few minutes, then his patience snapped.

'White water, that's what you saw. I'll teach you to waste my time,' and he swung a heavy fist at the boy's head.

Roger ducked just in time to avoid the blow, and the captain's fist crashed into the mast. He yelped with pain and looked at his bleeding knuckles. Of course, he put the blame on Roger. Muttering curses, he was about to thrash the greenhorn when Jiggs, seeing what was likely to happen, interrupted with a ringing shout:

'Bl-o-o — o-o-ws!'

The captain and Roger turned to look. There was no mistake about it this time. The boy's report had been right. The jet was four points on the weather-bow and it was the spout of a sperm-whale.

'All hands on deck!' roared the captain.

The call was repeated by the mate below: 'All hands on deck! Back the main yard! Stand by to lower!'

5
Nantucket Sleigh Ride

At once the ship came alive. There was the sound of heavy sea-boots on the deck as the men ran aft to the boats. The mate kept shouting orders. Again the captain turned upon Roger.

'Well, what are you doing here? Get down to the boats.'

Very willingly, Roger left the captain and scrambled down to the deck as fast as his gammy arm would permit. Durkins, the second mate, caught sight of him.

'You — I can use you in my boat. Third oar.'

The men leaped into the whale-boats. The lashings were cast off.

'Lower away!'

The falls raced through the sheaves. Down went the boats. The men bent to the oars. Three light cedar whale-boats, six men in each, streaked away towards the spouting whale.

'All right, boys,' shouted the mate, 'give way now and spring to it. Put some beef in it.'

Roger felt the mate's eye on him. He could guess what the mate was thinking. This greenhorn would probably catch a crab — get his oar fouled with the others.

Durkins relaxed when he saw that Roger knew how to handle an oar. The kid kept his eye on the stroke-oar and timed his own stroke with it. What the mate could not guess was how painful this was for Roger with the right arm singing from the blow of the belaying-pin.

The mate stood at the steering-sweep. He could not see the whale, and even the spout was hidden by intervening waves. Yet he knew where to steer. He kept glancing at the ship, which had turned its prow towards the whale.

He knew, too, when the whale was on the surface and when it dived. This information was signalled to him by the captain at the masthead. When the whale broke water the captain ran up a flag; when it 'went flukes', plunged beneath the surface, the flag was lowered.

Roger saw his brother in one of the other boats. Hal was pulling lustily. His boat was edging ahead. But Durkins was not to be easily beaten.

'Pull, boys. Pull like steers. Pull. Pile it on. Long and strong. Pull — every son of you. What's the matter, kid?'

This last remark was addressed to Roger, who was in such pain that he could no longer pull the fourteen-foot ash oar.

'My arm,' said Roger.

'And I don't wonder,' said Durkins, 'after the rap that pig gave you. Ship your oar.'

Roger took in his oar. He felt like a deserter. With only four oars working the boat steadily lost ground. Both the other boats passed it. Durkins still urged his men on, but it was hopeless. Roger knew how disappointed the second mate must be. Then his eye lit on the mast, which lay across the thwarts.

'I could put up the sail,' he suggested.

'No good,' said the mate. 'We're too close to the wind.'

Roger knew nothing about whaling, but a good deal about sailing. He did not want to argue with the mate. Testing the wind on his face, he felt that the sail would draw enough air to be worth while. They might even be able to overtake the other boats.

'Please, sir, may I try it?' he ventured.

The mate hesitated. 'Guess it will do no harm,' he said, and added rather bitterly: 'You're no good to us, anyway. You may as well be doing that as sitting there like a lump on a log.'

Roger lost no time in stepping the mast. Lifting it, he placed it erect in the hole in the forward thwart. The boom dropped. The triangular sail opened and hung like a tired dishcloth. The men muttered in disgust.

Roger hauled in on the sheet-rope. The sail suddenly filled with air and began to pull.

Roger handled the sheet like the rein of a race-horse, drawing a little, giving a little, to suit every changing whim of the breeze. The boat gained speed. Presently it was racing away like a scared cat. It was rapidly overhauling the other boats.

'The kid's got something,' said Durkins.

The whale was now in plain sight. Its great black

hulk blocked the sky. To Roger it looked as big as the ship. This little twenty-foot boat was only as long as the monster's lower jaw.

He realized fully for the first time the risk men take who go out in such an eggshell to attack the greatest living creature on the face of the earth. Excitement raced up and down his spine. He had to confess to himself that he was scared. He almost hoped that one of the other boats would get there first.

And that was what happened. The boat in which Hal was pulling shot up alongside the whale a split second before the mate's. The harpooner standing in the bow hurled his iron. In his hurry to be first he threw at too great a distance and the harpoon fell into the water.

At the same instant the mate's boat, propelled by both oars and sail, slid into position beside the whale just behind its enormous head. The harpooner was Jimson. Dropping his oar he leaped to his feet in the boat's bow, raised his harpoon and plunged it into the black hide.

The monster hardly felt it, for the iron 'boned' — that is, instead of penetrating deep into the flesh, it struck a bone, and with such force that the iron was bent. Then it dropped away into the sea.

At once Jimson snatched up his second iron and threw it with all his might. It sank in up to the hitches.

A tremor like an earthquake ran through the giant body.

'Stern all!' yelled the mate, and the men lost no time in rowing the boat backward out of reach of the whale's flukes. At the same time the enormous two-fluked tail, bigger than the screw of any vessel afloat, rose thirty feet into the air and came down again upon the water with a resounding crash not six inches from the gunwale of the boat. The wave made by this gigantic blow washed into the boat and half filled it.

Away went the sea giant, towing the boat behind it. The line from the harpoon to the boat was as taut as a tightrope. The boat was flying through the spray at a good twenty knots. Wave-tops kept tumbling in. The men shipped their oars and bailed for their lives.

A picture of the whole exciting operation was being taken by Mr Scott in the third boat. But it was only a few moments before the whale and the towed boat had disappeared behind the blue waves, tearing across the sea on what whalers choose to call the 'Nantucket sleigh ride'. Roger wondered if it was the last picture that would ever be taken of him. If they couldn't get the water out of the boat faster than it came in, they would all very soon be on their way down to visit Davy Jones.

6
Man Overboard

Suddenly the whale changed direction. The boat was yanked round to the right so forcibly that a man who had stood up to bail a bucket of water into the sea went over the side.

Roger was amazed that no one did anything about it.

'Man overboard!' he yelled.

Surely they would cut the tow-line, turn the boat about and go back to the rescue. But the mate gave no such order. He stood, gripping the steering-oar, gazing straight ahead at the speeding whale. The other men were equally silent. They kept on scooping out the water. The mate noticed that Roger had stopped work and was staring at him in astonishment.

'Bail, boy, bail!'

'But the man — '

'One of the other boats may pick him up. If not, it's his bad luck.' Seeing the shocked look on Roger's face the mate went on: 'You'll soon learn, boy. Whaling is a serious business. That big bull has a hundred barrels of oil in him. What d'ye think the captain would say if we let him go just to pick a man out of the water?'

Roger went back to bailing. He felt he was in a world of a hundred years ago. The whaling ship *Killer* stuck to the old traditions. Human life was cheap. What mattered was barrels of oil. Today, men who work are protected by many safety devices. In the old days a man must look out for himself and devil take him if he didn't look sharp. Today, we are quite careful not to kill one man at a time — we only plan to kill a hundred thousand or a million at one blow with a hydrogen bomb. Roger gave up trying to figure which were more cruel, the old days or the new.

Suddenly the line slackened. The whale had again changed direction. It was now coming straight for the boat.

It had not been able to get rid of its enemy by running away. Now it was going to attack.

It opened its enormous jaws, revealing a cavern big enough to take boat and all. It was like looking through the door into a room twenty feet long and twelve feet wide.

But it was not a comfortable-looking room. The floor was paved with sharp teeth a foot long and weighing as much as four pounds each. The upper jaw had no teeth, but a row of sockets into which the teeth of the lower jaw would fit when the mouth was closed. It would be too bad for the man or the boat that happened to get ground into one of those sockets like meal in a mortar.

Roger had learned enough about whales to know that the sperm is a man-eater and a boat-eater. It is quite different from the toothless baleen, or whalebone-whale, that has nothing in its mouth but a big sieve to catch the small creatures of the sea that are its food. Such a whale couldn't swallow a man, and wouldn't want to. It could take a thousand crayfish but wouldn't know what to do with a shark.

But the big sperm has no use for the little titbits that can be found on the surface of the sea. His favourite food is the enormous cuttle-fish sometimes fifty feet long and equipped with a great savage beak that may kill the whale or wound it so badly that it will carry the scars for the rest of its life.

Such a whale can swallow a man as easily as a man may swallow a pill. Many times whalers have found a shark twelve feet long or longer in the stomach of a sperm-whale.

'Lay to the oars!' yelled the mate.

The men left bailing to row. The boat had not yet lost the momentum of its swift flight over the sea. This, helped by the rowing, carried it forward fast enough, so that when the whale arrived the boat was no longer there. It barely missed the jaws, which closed on the steering-oar, crunching it to bits.

Away went the whale, only to turn and come back again towards the boat. This time it dived, as if planning to come up beneath the boat and toss it into the air.

'Hang on!' shouted the mate.

The men clutched the gunwales and waited for the shock.

Now all could look forward to being dumped into the sea. Blood from the wound made by the harpoon had stained the water and attracted sharks. Roger suddenly realized that the man who had fallen overboard back there where there were no sharks and no angry whale was the lucky one after all.

The blow from beneath did not come. Instead, the line began to sing out of the tub in which it was coiled.

'He sounds!' said Durkins.

Roger heard no sound. Then he realized what Durkins had meant. When a whale 'sounds', it means that he dives deep. A strange word, when you come to think of it. A sounding whale makes no sound. On the surface he may have been blowing and splashing and champing his great jaws, and even groaning with pain, but when he dives you hear nothing. Nothing but the whirr of the line out of the tub as the great beast carries the harpoon deeper and deeper.

'Look out for that line!' commanded the mate. The flying line lashed about like an angry snake. If an arm or leg got caught in it the limb would be nipped off as neatly as if amputated by a surgeon's saw. Either that, or the man would be snatched out of the boat by the whizzing line and carried down after the whale.

How deep would the whale go? The sperm-whale is the best diver on earth. With the greatest of ease he can go a quarter of a mile or more straight down.

A man would be crushed to a pulp long before

he could reach such a depth. The pressure of the water upon his body would squeeze all the flesh out from between his bones and crush his skull. Even if he could descend to such a depth he could not rise again to the surface without getting a terrific case of the 'bends' that would cost him his life.

The line was nearly all gone from the tub. But there was a second tub of line, and a sailor hastily tied the two ends together. In a few seconds the first tub was empty, and the line was whirring out of the second so fast that the eye could not follow it.

'He can't go much deeper,' said one of the men.

'Can't he, though?' retorted the mate. 'Ever hear what happened down near Panama. A submarine cable broke and a repair-ship was sent out to fix it. When the ship hauled the two broken ends to the surface a dead sperm-whale was found in the coils. That cable had been lying on the bottom of the sea, and the sea at that point is half a mile deep. To get caught in the cable, the whale had to dive half a mile straight down.'

'We can't afford to have this one dive so deep,' said the man who had spoken before. 'We have only three hundred fathoms of line.'

'Better start snubbing,' said the mate.

A sailor threw two loops of the line around a loggerhead, or post. The line still ran, but it was slowed by friction against the post and this increased the drag on the whale. The monster might even be discouraged from his downward dive.

This snubbing could be dangerous. If the line

was too tight round the post the whale might drag boat and all beneath the sea. The bow was already much lower and the gunwales were awash. Men bailed lustily as waves broke into the boat.

There was still another danger — fire. The friction of the line against the loggerhead sent up a curl of blue smoke and presently a yellow flame sputtered.

'Douse it!' ordered the mate.

The man nearest the loggerhead emptied his leather bailing-bucket over the flame. It disappeared, and so did the smoke. But it was only a few moments before the heat of the passing line started a new blaze. Again and again the loggerhead had to be baptized with sea-water.

7
A Quarter of a Mile Down

The line went slack.

The big bull had ended his dive. Perhaps he thought he had gone deep enough to be safe, perhaps he had been slowed down by the pull of the line. He lay there more than a quarter of a mile deep while five men in a boat anxiously waited.

'How long can they stay down?' Roger asked.

Roger remembered his own underwater experiences. When diving in the pearl lagoon he had been able to hold his breath for three minutes. No human diver could do much better than that.

'No telling,' said the mate. 'Usually fifteen to forty minutes. But they've been known to stay below for an hour and a half.'

'How can they do without air for so long?'

'You saw all that spouting,' replied the mate. 'Every time he spouted he blew out dead air and took in fresh air. He did that about a dozen times. That wasn't just to fill his lungs – it was to put oxygen into his blood. That's where it counts. And a whale can do about five times as good a job of oxygenating its blood as a man can do. No other breathing animal can do as well. A living submarine, that's what a whale is.'

The other whale-boats had come up, ready to help if they were needed. The man who had tumbled overboard had been rescued and now climbed back into the mate's boat.

He was soaking wet and worn out, but he got no sympathy from the crew. Whalers had no kind words for a man who was too clumsy to keep his balance in a boat.

He shivered with cold. Roger stripped off his sweater and gave it to him. The men laughed at him for taking clothes from a boy. Angrily, he gave the sweater back to Roger. He would rather shiver than be laughed at.

For more than three-quarters of an hour they waited. The men sat idly in the bobbing boats. One would think they would be glad of the rest. But every moment was full of suspense.

No one could say where the monster would come up. He might rise beneath the boats, tossing them high into the air and spilling their occupants into the shark-infested waters.

'The longer he stays down the faster he'll come up,' said the mate. 'He'll be crazy for fresh air.'

The sea began to boil. It was as if a great fire had been lit under it. It rose in a high bubbling hump, and up through this hill of water shot the whale as if he had been fired from a gun.

He rose clear out of the water and seemed to be standing on his tail like a black tower eighty feet high — about the height of a seven-storey building.

Imagine seeing a skyscraper suddenly appear on the open sea. It was a spectacle to remember, and Scott operating his ciné-camera was making sure that it would be remembered.

Down came the skyscraper, sending out waves that dashed the boats into each other and made the men bail furiously. The whale threw up one white palm tree after another as he breathed out stale air and took in fresh. It would take him many minutes to restore oxygen to his blood, and during that time he would think of nothing else. This was the whalers' chance.

'Lay to it, boys,' shouted the mate. 'Pull! Come in just behind his left eye.'

He left the stern and stepped over the thwarts to the bow, while the harpooner came back and took his place in the stern.

It was the old custom. The officer must have the honour of killing the whale. Durkins took up the lance. It was an iron spear five feet long and as sharp as a razor. It was quite unlike the harpoon. The harpoon was made to go in and hang on, like a fish-hook. The lance was made to go much farther in, and kill.

The mate stood in the bow, the lance held high in his right hand.

'Closer,' he ordered.

Roger would have been willing not to get any closer to the great black boat-slasher. His heart was in his mouth. The enormous hulk of the whale loomed above the small boat and shut off half the sky. The fountains of steam blasted off into the sky like the exhaust of a jet plane.

Now the bow actually touched the black hide. The mate leaned forward and plunged the lance in just behind the eye.

'Back her, back her!' he yelled.

The boat pulled away. The whole body of the whale was trembling and twisting. A deep groan came from the monster, reminding those who listened that this was no fish, but a mammal like the man who was killing him. The groan began on a low tone, but rose to a high wailing bellow.

Then again he spouted. This time the palm tree was not white, but red with blood. This the whalemen called 'flowering'. And it did look like a gigantic flower, thirty feet high. It was evident that the lance had pierced the lungs. Roger shrank as the rain of blood fell on the boats, but the men were cheering.

'A hundred barrels if he's a pint!' exulted Jimson.

The whale was dead. The sea was blood-red and the sharks were already tearing at the carcass.

A line was put over the tail and the three boats joined forces in hauling the prize back to the ship.

It was a long, slow job. Fifteen oars dipped and pulled. Each pull won only an inch or two. The captain could have brought the ship closer, but he seemed to take a perverse delight in seeing the oarsmen sweat it out. It was long after dark before the whale was alongside the ship. There the cable round the tail was passed aboard and secured. It was as if two ships lay side by side.

The boats were hoisted to the davits and the men collapsed on deck, quite exhausted. The cook

brought them meat and coffee. Roger said to Jimson:
'Boy, won't that bunk feel good!'

8
The Wolves of the Sea

There was great turmoil in the water around the dead whale. The sea was alive with sharks rushing frantically about, taking bites out of the carcass and out of each other.

'That won't do,' growled the captain. 'By morning we won't have any whale left. Somebody's got to get down there and fend off those sharks. Who volunteers?'

No one volunteered. Even if they had been fresh none of them would have chosen to spend the night on that slippery carcass fighting off the wolves of the sea.

Captain Grindle walked about among his weary sailors. His eye lit on Roger. The captain's fist was still sore from the whack against the mast when Roger had dodged his blow.

'You — you young squirt!' snapped Grindle. 'Get down on that whale.'

Hal spoke up. 'Let me go.' Mr Scott also ventured to protest. The mate said:

'The kid's pretty well whacked, Captain. He pulled a good oar. He deserves to rest.'

'Who gives orders on this ship?' roared the skipper. 'Did ever a ship have such a pack of softies! The next man who talks back at me will be put in irons.'

He gave Roger a hard kick in the ribs.

'Get down there, you lazy loafer. This ought to be good — a gent dancing on a whale's back. You may find the dance-floor a bit slippery. One good thing about it —if we lose you, we won't lose much. I can't spare a real man. Get along!'

He kicked again, but since Roger had already moved away the captain lost his footing and sat down hard on the deck. Some of the men laughed. That did not improve the captain's temper. Hurling curses about him like belaying-pins, he strode off to his quarters aft.

Roger stood at the rail looking down on the dead monster besieged by sharks. An almost full moon lit the weird scene. The mate was looping a rope around Roger beneath the arms. The other end of the rope would be held by a seaman on deck.

'If you slip, he'll pull you up,' said the mate.

The seaman, whose name was Brad, did not willingly accept the job.

'Look here,' he complained. 'This ain't my watch. I'm tired. I've done my bit.'

'So has everybody else,' replied the mate. 'You know well enough there aren't any watches when we catch a whale.'

'But suppose I fall asleep?'

'Don't,' warned the mate.

He gave Roger a whaling-spade. This was a flat razor-edged knife about the same shape as a spade fastened to the end of a fifteen-foot pole.

Tomorrow, spades like this would be used to cut the blubber from the whale. Tonight, the spade would be Roger's only weapon against the sharks.

'Try to punch them in the nose,' the mate instructed. 'That's where they kill easiest. Or rip them in the belly when they turn over.'

Roger, trembling with weariness, but stimulated to new strength by this new challenge, climbed over the rail. Brad eased out the line and Roger was lowered to the whale's back.

Roger's first act was to fall flat on his face. The captain had not been fooling. The whale's back was slippery. It was more slippery than any dance-floor.

The whale's skin is not wrinkled like an elephant's or rhino's. It is not hairy like the hide of a buffalo or lion. It has no scales like those of a fish. It is as smooth as glass.

Worse than that, it is like greased glass. Oil from the blubber beneath it oozes up through it, filling the pores so as to keep out the cold and enable the monster to slide through the water like a stream-lined submarine. Roger heard a low chuckle from the sailor Brad, watching him from the deck above. He crawled to his feet, clutching the spade. The ocean swell rolled the whale gently from side to side. At each roll Roger slid, and Brad chuckled.

If Roger slipped down on the off-side he would be promptly finished off by sharks. If he slid down on the other side he would be crushed between the ship and the whale. The danger terrified Roger, but the man above him couldn't care less.

Brad resented being posted on this dreary night

duty. He was already tired of holding the rope-end. Glancing round to make sure that no officer was looking, he made fast the end of the line to a stay. Then he settled himself to enjoy the acrobatics of the moonlit figure on the rolling dance-floor.

Roger was not going to give him much amusement. The boy was learning how to keep his footing. With his sharp spade he cut two footholds in which he could sink his heels. Now he swayed with the role, but did not slip. With his feet firmly planted, and the rope to hang on to, he could stay upright.

Brad was disappointed. It had promised to be a good show, but the boy had spoiled it. Disgusted, Brad slumped down to the deck and went to sleep.

The jar made by a big wave sent Roger sliding and he got back to his footholds with difficulty.

'Hi,' he called. 'Will you hold that line a little tighter?'

He got no answer. He called again, without effect. He saw that the line had been looped to a stay. He supposed that Brad had sneaked off to his bunk.

The silence terrified Roger. The silent sky above with stars racing back and forth as the whale rolled, the silent ship, the silent sea hiding mystery and death.

Only the dorsal fin of each shark could be seen. It stood up like a little black sail in the path of the moon. There were at least a dozen of these small black sails speeding here and there, now rushing in to the whale's flank, now sailing away again as

the shark swam off with a chunk of meat in its teeth to swallow at leisure.

As one sail approached, Roger plunged in his spade and felt it go deep into the living ship beneath that sail. At once blood poured from the injured shark while its tail savagely thrashed the water in an effort to escape. But the other sharks were upon it at once and, like the cannibals they were, proceeded to tear their companion to bits and devour him.

When they had done dining upon their brother they turned their attention once more to the whale. Another sail came flying in, but disappeared at the last moment as the shark turned upside-down before taking its bite. Some sharks prefer this upside-down way of attack. Roger's cutting-spade plunged into the brute's throat. Again the sharks forgot the whale to turn upon their injured companion.

Why did they prefer to eat each other? It was because they were blood-lovers. Blood is to sharks what alcohol is to men. They go wild over it, drunk even at the smell of it. And it is much easier to get through the skin to the blood of a shark than to penetrate a whale's coat of blubber a foot thick and reach its arteries and heart.

If Roger could just keep these cannibals feeding upon each other he could save the whale. He tried every time to strike the sensitive nose. Often this was impossible and he sliced into the shark as it was swimming away. When the cut was far back towards the tail where the shark could reach it by turning its head back and tail forward, this strange devil of the sea would actually tear at the wound with its teeth, drink its own blood and devour its own flesh.

The red sea attracted more and more sharks. Many of them attacked out of reach of Roger's fifteen-foot spade. He must be able to run forward towards the whale's head, or back towards its tail. Two footholds were not enough — he had to cut a row of them, both forward and aft, each hole cupped two or three inches deep into the hide. Along this curious path on a whale's back Roger ran this way and that as far as the length of his rope would permit, and stabbed every attacker he could reach.

Once as the whale rolled he slipped out of the tracks and slid far over until his feet were in the sea. With a rush the savage beasts closed in on him, snapping at his boots. Fortunately they were tough and strong, and not easily crushed.

Then one boot was yanked off together with the woollen sock beneath it.

Roger felt teeth closing upon his bare leg. He jerked it out of the way and hauled himself up on to the whale by means of the rope.

Blood streamed from his leg. Should he climb on deck and have it attended to? There was no surgeon on board. It was usual for the captain to have some skill in first aid. But Roger would rather suffer the pain and risk of blood-poisoning than submit himself to the tender mercies of Captain Grindle.

He scrubbed the wound with sea-water, tied his

handkerchief round the leg and went on with his work.

Midnight came and went. Roger had trouble in keeping his eyes open. A ghostly haze lay over the sea. It was the time of night for men to sleep and ghosts to walk. Roger was not superstitious, but he could not help but be affected by the mystery of the night.

And then he saw something that sent a chill of fear down his spine. It could not be true. He must have gone to sleep and he was having a terrible nightmare.

For the dorsal fins that cut the water, each of them about a foot high, had suddenly grown into great black sails as tall as a man. Taller — they were certainly seven or eight feet high.

No more did they skim along gently like sail-boats. They shot by at furious speed. They ploughed up the water and sent spray high into the air.

One of them came straight towards the whale. It struck the great eighty-foot monster with such force that Roger felt the vibration throughout the huge body. No shark, not even the great white shark, could strike such a blow.

9
Fighting Killer-Whales

Then one of these impossible monsters raised its head six feet above the surface of the sea. It looked like a great black torpedo standing on end. It was as big as a dozen sharks. Evidently supported by the moving tail and fins beneath, it continued to stand up like a statue for many seconds. And it looked straight at Roger.

The moon in its westward journey was now in position to light the beast's eyes. Roger had never seen such eyes. They were not small like those of a whale. They were as big as saucers, and round and staring. Roger felt as small as a midget under that terrible gaze.

And he realized that he was not dreaming. He was looking at a killer-whale.

The killer-whale is the most dangerous creature of the sea. Curiously enough it is not really a whale. It is the largest of the porpoise family. But sailors of the early days gave it the name killer-whale, and the name has stuck.

A famous scientist has called it 'the most terrible flesh-eating creature on our planet'. A full-grown killer-whale is about thirty feet long. It is shaped like a torpedo and can flash through the water at a speed of thirty-six miles per hour. It has a dozen huge sharp teeth in the lower jaw and another dozen in the upper. The teeth are curved inward, and whatever they take hold of has very little chance of escape.

The big eyes have keen vision and behind them is an intelligent brain. In fact, the brain of the killer-whale is said to be better than that of the chimpanzee, better than that of any other living thing except man.

But unhappily that wonderful brain has only one ambition — to kill. It is the brain of a devil. No wonder the Eskimos who believe in evil spirits call this beast a wicked god that can take on the form of a killer-whale in the water or a wolf on land.

Killers are clever. When they see walruses or seals lying on a floating cake of ice, they will come up under the floe and break it to bits so that the animals will fall into the water. They will go after men in the same deadly fashion. Cherry Garrett in *The Worst Journey in the World* tells of what happened on an Antarctic expedition when a man and two dogs on an ice-floe were attacked by seven killer-whales: 'The next moment the whole floe under him and the dogs heaved up and split into fragments. One could hear the booming noise as the whales rose under the ice and struck it with their backs. Whale after whale rose under the ice setting it rocking fearfully. Luckily Ponting kept his feet and was able to fly to security. By an extraordinary chance also, the splits had been made around and between the dogs so that neither of them fell into the water. Then it was clear that the whales shared our astonishment, for one after another, their huge hideous heads shot vertically into the air through the cracks which they had made. As they reared them to a height of six or eight feet it was possible to see their tawny head markings, their glistening eyes and the terrible array of teeth, the most terrifying in the world. But the fact that they could display such deliberate cunning, that they were able to break ice of such thickness, at least two feet, and that they could act in unison, was a revelation to us.'

Sometimes instead of coming up under the ice a killer will slide up on top of it, clear of the water, grab its prey, then wriggle off into the sea. In the same way it may come aboard a raft, a whale-boat or a small ship.

Recently a tuna-boat off the California coast was visited by a killer. It circled round and round the boat until the ship's cook got annoyed and potted the beast with a rifle bullet.

Instead of killing it or scaring it away, the bullet only made the killer furiously angry. He swam straight for the ship, shot up into the air and crashed head-on into the galley, the great jaws chopping the cookhouse into kindling. Luckily the cook saved himself by diving head-first into the hold.

The killer thrashed savagely about, breaking all the dishes and crunching the iron pans and buckets until they looked as if a tractor had run over them. He chewed up the galley stove, fire and all, but when a huge pot containing enough soup for twenty men spilled its boiling contents on his nose he flipped back into the sea and swam off.

The cook crawled up, green and shaking, from the hold and looked at the ruins of his galley. The crew ate cold salt pork that day. The cook never again fired a bullet at a killer-whale.

One after another the killers sat up in the sea and looked at Roger. He knew they could easily slide up on the whale's back. Then — one crunch — and Hal would have no brother.

Perhaps he had better swarm up to the safety of the deck while there was still a chance. But if he ran away the killers would devour the whale. Already they were making savage lunges at the body and swimming off with great chunks of flesh. Several of them were attacking the head. Roger remembered hearing, on his Pacific voyages, of the killer's habit of forcing the whale's mouth open to get at its tongue.

Luckily this was a sperm whale, not a baleen.

Nothing tasted so good to a killer as a baleen's tongue. It was also valuable to the whaler, since it contained fifteen barrels of the finest oil.

The sperm's tongue was small and dry by comparison. Yet if Roger allowed these thieves to get away with even that, he hated to think what would happen to him at the hands of Captain Grindle.

The great carcass quivered and shook as the savages knocked their noses against the lips in an effort to open the mouth and get at the tongue. Whatever Roger was going to do he would have to do quickly. His rope was not long enough to allow him to get to the whale's head.

With more courage than common sense he threw off the rope and started forward. He cut holes for his feet. Even with the help of these footholds he had trouble in keeping his balance. The big whale rolled with the waves and trembled under the attack of the killers.

Roger was now on the whale's head. The head of a sperm-whale is an enormous box some ten feet high. The nose is on top of it and the mouth is under it. So Roger stood many feet above the killers as they battered against the whale's lips. Fortunately they were too busy trying to break into this big food-box to pay much attention to the small morsel of boy above them. So long as he left them alone they might leave him alone.

He could not afford to let them alone. But what could he do with a spade when even a rifle bullet would have no effect upon such a beast?

He believed that the spade could do what the bullet could not. The spade would let out blood. If these monsters had as bad table manners as the sharks, they would attack their bloody brother. He hoped it would work. There was nothing else he could do.

With all his strength he drove the sharp spade down into the head of the nearest killer. The tremendous thrashing that resulted scared him out of his wits. The animal he had wounded backed off, raised his head man-high out of the sea and stared full at Roger. Then he submerged and came in with a rush. Close to the whale he shot up out of the water and on to the big head.

Roger had not waited for him. He had lost no

time in running aft. The killer's jaws clamped upon emptiness.

With one wrench of its body the angry beast twisted its head close to the boy. Blood spurting from the wound sprayed upon Roger. He hunted for the rope by which he could pull himself up to the deck. Dawn was now greying the sky and in its light he could see that the precious rope had swung out of reach against the side of the ship.

He shouted for help. Brad woke, rose and looked sleepily over the rail. He could not believe what he saw. His mouth hung open stupidly as he tried to clear the mist of sleep from his brain.

'Throw me a line!' yelled Roger.

The big killer was squirming like a fish out of water, trying to get near enough to close its jaws upon its enemy. Then a line came whistling over Roger's shoulder. It was not the stupid Brad who had thrown it, but the second mate, Durkins.

'Latch on to it, boy!'

Roger immediately gripped the line and had his arms almost pulled out of their sockets, so powerful was the pull of the mate's strong arms as he hauled in on the line. Roger's swinging body crashed into the ship's side, but how good that felt in comparison with the crunch of the killer's teeth! A moment later he was spilled on the deck. He got unsteadily to his feet.

'Are you all right, boy?'

'I'm all right,' said Roger, but he was still dizzy from the nerve-racking experience of the last few moments. 'The killers are after the tongue,' he said.

'Don't worry about that,' said the mate. 'You fixed it so they won't get it. Good job, kid.'

Roger was not so sure that he had fixed it. Five killers were still struggling to get their heads into the whale's mouth. In the meantime the wounded killer twisted himself off the whale's back and fell heavily into the sea. The blood spread out over the waves. It attracted his companions. They rushed in upon the wounded animal, churning the sea, gulping the blood, taking great bites out of the flukes, the fins, the lips. They would not stop until there was nothing left but the skeleton.

'It will keep them out of mischief for an hour,' said the mate with satisfaction. 'That will give us time to get the stage out.' He turned towards the fo'c'sle and bawled: 'All hands on deck!'

The men came tumbling up. With them was Hal, who had spent a sleepless night worrying about his young brother. Scott came from his cabin aft. Both of them would have been glad to spend the night helping the boy, but their interference would only have got him as well as themselves into trouble. Now they were eager to hear about his experiences. They talked, over the brief breakfast of coffee and hard-tack.

Their conversation was cut short by the appearance of Captain Grindle.

'Everybody loafing as usual,' he snarled. 'And a whale waiting to be cut in.'

He fixed his eye on Roger.

'I thought I posted you on the carcass. Who told you to come up?'

'I hauled him up, sir,' said the mate.

'Well, get him down again.'

Durkins ventured to object. 'It isn't necessary, sir. He sliced a killer. That will keep the other killers busy. As for the sharks, the killers scared them away.'

The captain peered over the rail at the surge of savage beasts enjoying their blood breakfast.

'Then what are you waiting for?' shouted the captain. 'Get out the cutting-stage. Hop to it!'

He had forgotten about Roger. Durkins spoke in the boy's ear.

'Get to your bunk. Quick, before he spots you.'

Roger slipped forward and down into the fo'c'sle. The boards of his bunk felt like feathers. He promptly lost himself in beautiful, delicious, heavenly sleep.

10
Cat-O'-Nine-Tails

Captain Grindle turned upon Hal.

'Well, if it ain't the Gent!' he sneered. 'Your softie brother got his. Pretty soon I'll be getting around to you.'

'I hope you do,' Hal answered. 'That would be better than taking it out on the boy.'

Grindle glared. 'Do you question my authority?'

'I question your intelligence.' Hal knew he was unwise to say it but he was too angry to guard his tongue.

Grindle's always prominent eyes now seemed to stand straight out from his head. He could not believe what he had heard. He pushed his face close to Hal's and said in a low, rasping voice:

'Do I understand you proper? You say that I don't know how to handle my crew?'

'Of course you don't,' Hal replied. He knew that he had waded in too far. He would have been glad to wade out again, but it was too late. He might as well go deeper. 'A man who would do what you did last night to that boy is not fit to give orders to anyone.'

The captain started back as if he had been struck.

He stood like a man turned to stone. Then he came to life and bawled: 'Mr Durkins!' in a voice that made everybody jump.

The mate came running.

'String this fellow up,' ordered the captain. 'Strip him to the waist. We'll put a pattern on his back that will stay there if he lives to be a hundred.'

The order took the mate by surprise, but he did not dare object.

'Aye, aye, sir,' he answered, 'right now, if you say so. But perhaps you'll be wanting us to get in the blubber first before the killers make off with it.'

Grindle looked over the rail. The cannibals were still breakfasting on their companion, but soon they would be done with him and free to attack the big whale.

'Of course,' he said. 'Business first, then pleasure. And what a party we'll have when the work is done! Something to look forward to, eh, Gent?' He turned and strode aft.

The mate scowled at Hal.

'Now you've done it. Why in the devil's name couldn't you keep your mouth shut? Don't expect me to get you out of this.'

'I won't,' Hal said. 'I got myself into it.'

He could not be sorry. The captain's brutality towards Roger was enough to make anyone rebel. And yet perhaps he had only made things worse for Roger by speaking up. As for himself, he could already feel the cut of the cat-o'-nine-tails into his flesh.

The cutting-stage was now lowered. This was a sort of platform that was lashed to the rail of the ship when not in use. When let down it projected about ten feet from the ship like a balcony. Directly under it was the whale.

The cutters went out on the stage. Each was armed with one of the long-handled spades. With these sharp tools they cut a foot deep into the whale's hide, making a lengthwise slit. Then one man descended to the whale's back and fixed a large 'blubber-hook' in the hide. A line ran from the blubber-hook up over a block in the rigging and down to the windlass.

The man who had fixed the hook clambered back to safety and the mate shouted: 'Haul!'

Then men heaved on the windlass. The rope tightened. The strong pull of the hook lifted the whale an inch or two higher in the water. It had a greater effect upon the ship. The weight of the monster made the vessel lean farther and farther to starboard until it was hard to keep a footing on the slippery deck.

Then there was a tearing sound and the hook went up carrying a great strip of hide with it. As the whale rolled the hide peeled like the skin of an orange. Whalers called this the blanket. It was a good name. This hide, a foot thick, consisting mainly of oily blubber, wrapped the whale as in a blanket and kept it snug and warm when it sank into the chill depths of the sea.

The piece of blanket was hauled inboard and dropped on the deck. The process was repeated and, piece by piece, the entire blanket of the whale was brought aboard.

The hardest job came next. The head must be

cut off. The spades attacked the neck, cutting deeper and deeper through muscle and nerve and flesh. Every once in a while the blades, dulled by bones, had to be resharpened. They must be so sharp that they would slice through the bones and even through the backbone itself.

At last the head and trunk parted company. The carcass was now cast loose and drifted several hundred feet off, where a company of sharks attacked it.

Now it was a race with the killers. They had almost finished off their dead friend. They began making passes at the whale's head, trying again to get at the tongue.

The head, still floating in the sea but secured by hooks, was turned upside-down. Cutters neatly removed the lower jaw. And there, exposed to view, was the elephant-size tongue.

It was severed at the root, a hook was fixed in it, the windlass creaked, and the great spongy morsel so loved by the killers began to rise. It was none too soon. Already the killers were nipping at it feverishly. Several large bites were torn out of it. Even when it was eight feet above the sea three killers stood up on their tails snapping at it. Then it was drawn out of their reach and hauled aboard.

It would have done Roger good to hear how the men cheered. The rich fine oil of the tongue would put more money into the pocket of every man aboard. 'Don't forget,' said Jimson, 'we owe it to the kid. Fifteen barrels in that tongue if there's a pint!'

The disappointed killers turned upon the floating carcass. They scared away the sharks, but they could not scare away the frigate birds, albatrosses and gulls that had come in swarms to this royal feast.

The cutters were not done with the head. It contained another rich prize. Having turned it right side up a cutter with a rope about his waist stood on the head and poked about with his spade, hunting for the soft spot. When he found it he cut a round opening about two feet across.

A bucket was let down through the hole and came up full of clear oil as sweet-smelling as any perfume. Bucketful after bucketful was hoisted to the deck and poured into casks. For this oil was so pure that it did not need to be boiled in the try-pots.

When the job was finished the mate did some adding up.

'Two thousand gallons of oil we got out of that head!'

Now the head itself was hoisted aboard. Even without the tongue and empty of oil it was so heavy that its weight listed the whaler far to starboard. When it lay at last on the deck it seemed as big as a cabin. Hal had to look up to see the top of it. He had known that a sperm-whale's head is one-third of the entire body, but it was hard to believe such a thing without actually seeing it.

Then came the dirty, greasy job of trying-out. The head and hide were cut into small pieces and dumped into the try-pots. As fast as the oil was boiled out of the blubber it was ladled out into casks.

Then the scraps of blubber from which the oil had been boiled were thrown out on deck. Hal wondered why they were not tossed overboard.

He soon saw why. When the fire burned low no more wood was put on it. Instead, the scraps of boiled-out blubber were thrown in. Thus blubber boiled blubber. The whale was actually cooking itself.

This saved both money and space. There would not be room on a ship for the wood required to boil down all the whales captured on an average voyage. Besides, it would be costly. But the scraps were supplied free of charge by every whale that came aboard.

Because of their oiliness they made an extremely hot fire. But it was not as pleasant as a wood fire. It sent up a greasy smudge of rank-smelling black smoke that made the men choke and gag and cover their faces with grey masks. Sweat running down their cheeks made rivers of white through the grey.

As the knives attacked the blubber, spurts of oily blood spattered the shirts and trousers of the workers. Some of them saved their clothes by taking them off and stowing them, and worked almost naked. Their bodies were rapidly covered by layers of grease and grime and blood. It got into their unshaven whiskers and uncut hair.

They were the sort of creatures one might see in a nightmare. They were pictures no artist could paint. If one of them had appeared suddenly in a Honolulu street women and children would have run screaming to their homes.

And the crew could not look forward to soap and

a hot shower when the job was finished. Water was too precious to be used to clean bodies that would only become dirty again. Most of the mess could be scraped off with the back edge of a knife, and the rest would wear off.

No, trying-out was not a pleasant job on an old-fashioned whaler. Yet the men went at it with a will, because every additional pint of oil meant more money in their pockets at the end of the voyage.

Hal, slipping on the fat-slimy deck, hacking at the blubber blanket with a long knife, shutting his eyes when the stuff spurted into his face, coughing in the oil smoke, was as grey, greasy and grubby as anyone else on board.

This was not his idea of a good time. How delighted he and his brother had been when their father proposed to let them go on a number of scientific expeditions, skipping a year of school because they were both too young for their classes. They were thrilled with the prospect of a whole year of hunting, fishing and exploring. And a lot of it so far had been great fun. But Hal had not looked forward to anything like this — drowning in a sea of oil and blood and smoke, with nothing to look forward to when the job was finished but a cat-o'-nine-tails.

Any hope that the captain had forgotten about the flogging was dispelled when Hal heard Grindle say to the mate:

'What man o' yours has the strongest right arm?'

'Well, Bruiser throws the hardest harpoon.'

Bruiser was a great brute with the strength of a gorilla. The mate might have made a different answer if he had known that the captain was not thinking of harpooning.

'Good,' said Grindle. 'He's the one to swing the cat.'

'You mean, you still aim to string up Hunt?'

'Of course!' snapped Grindle. 'Did you ever know me to go back on a promise?'

The mate felt like saying: You never go back on a bad promise. Just on good ones. He did not say it. He only thought it.

'I'll tell Bruiser,' he said.

11
The Great Bull

A cry came from the masthead.

'Whale away! Sparms on the lee bow! They blow! They blow!'

The captain went up the mainmast like an electrified monkey. He had no time now to think of 'the Gent'. Hal must wait for his flogging. Hal was almost sorry. He would rather have had it over and done with than be for ever looking forward to it.

The men piled into the boats. The tackle creaked and groaned as the boats descended from the davits and struck the bouncing waves.

'Cast off!' came the call. 'Oars — all together! Jump to it! Stroke — stroke — stroke!'

The spouts could be plainly seen. It was not just one whale this time, but a whole pod.

Funny, the names we give to various groups of animals. We speak of a flock of sheep, a herd of cattle, a gaggle of geese, a pride of lions, a school of fish — and a pod of whales.

It was hard to tell how many whales were in this pod. Perhaps half a dozen. Two of the spouts were very short, indicating that they came from babies.

Possibly all the animals in the group were of one family.

In Hal's boat the third mate, a small man named Brown, stood at the steering-sweep. At the bow-oar was the big, gorilla-like fellow, once a boxer, whom the men called Bruiser. When the time came he would rise from his seat and throw the harpoon.

Brown was small, but he had courage. He steered the boat into the very centre of the pod of whales.

'Steady now,' he said. 'Quiet with those oars. Don't alarm the beasties.'

The boat crept in between the two largest whales, probably the father and mother of the two youngsters. The other two whales might be uncles or aunts or just hangers-on.

Still unaware of the boat, the mother was giving milk to one of the youngsters. This is done in much the same way as a cow feeds a calf. But it is not quite as easy. If the baby whale were to try to take its breakfast under the whale it would not be able to breathe and would drown. Therefore the mother rolls over on her side to bring the nipples near the surface. The baby takes a nipple in its mouth and at the same time can keep its nostrils above water.

The greatest difference between a cow and a whale is that the cow gives milk only if the calf works to get it, but the baby whale does not have to work. The mother is equipped with a pump — a set of strong muscles which literally pump the milk into the infant.

When the baby's mouth slipped aside for a moment, Hal saw a great jet of white milk shoot out over the waves with the force of a stream from a fire-hose. The baby hastily fastened on again so that no more of the precious liquid would be lost.

Perhaps Nature made this unique pumping arrangement because it would take too long for the infant to get its breakfast by ordinary methods. The baby should have about two hundred pounds of milk a day. The new-born whale may be anywhere from fourteen to twenty-five feet long. It is without exception the biggest baby in the world. A lot of milk is needed to fill such a whale of a baby. If it had to pull for every drop it might easily become discouraged and fail to get the amount of food it needs for its rapidly growing body.

And how fast it does grow on this milk, much like cow's milk but extra rich in minerals, proteins and fats. The weight of the infant whale increases by nearly ten pounds every hour, two hundred and forty pounds a day! Within a year it doubles its length. At the age of four it becomes a mother or father.

The boat crept into the centre of this family group. The eyesight of whales is not very good and the monsters were still unaware of their danger. Their extremely keen ears did not detect any sound, for the men did not speak and dipped their oars silently.

Then Bruiser took up the harpoon. The haft of it touched the gunwale of the boat and made a faint click.

That was enough. At once the mother threw a protecting flipper over the baby, gave a spout of alarm, and turned to face the boat. The great bull struck the water with his flukes.

'Harpoon!' yelled Brown. 'Quick!'

Bruiser was both quick and strong. The harpoon went from his hand as if shot from a gun. It sank deep into the neck of the enormous male.

Bruiser, who looked like a giant among other men, was a dwarf beside this monster. And yet his arm, as big as a pin in comparison with one flipper, had made an earthquake go shivering through the huge black mountain of flesh. Man can move mountains, it is said, and Bruiser had done it.

12
The Giant Nutcracker

Hal braced himself for a sleigh ride. Surely the beast would take off on a wild race, towing the boat behind it as the previous catch had done?

But this bull had a family to take care of. He was not going to desert them. He wheeled about and came for the boat. He sent up a spout that reminded Hal of the launching of a satellite. The roar was like the blast of a jet when it breaks the sound barrier. Up and up went the column, house-high, then spread out like the leaves of a palm, and the spray falling from it sprinkled the men in the boat.

Now the two monsters both came head-on towards the boat. The two enormous heads were like the jaws of a giant nutcracker. Between them the stout cedar whale-boat would be crushed as easily as a walnut.

'Pull, pull!' shouted Brown. 'Pull for your lives!'

Five men pulled as they had never pulled before. Hal's oar cracked with the strain he put upon it.

The boat slid out from between two oncoming battering-rams. The forehead of a sperm-whale is straight up and down and some ten feet high. Now these two black cliffs met in a crash that sent a shiver through both great bodies and must have resulted in two whale-sized headaches.

The mother whale lay trembling, sheltering her babies under her flippers, one on each side. The big bull, infuriated by his failure to smash the boat and maddened by the pain of the harpoon in his neck, thrashed the water into white foam. The two who might have been uncles, for they both seemed to be males, swam round and round, blowing furiously and keeping the other two boats from entering the circle. Mr Scott, standing up in one boat, was getting a picture of the whole great show.

The big bull submerged and the water was suddenly quiet. Hal could see the long black body like a submarine passing just below the boat. He saw the tail whipping upward.

Then the world flew apart. The boat rose into the sky as if being hauled up by unseen cables. It turned upside down. Hal and his companions were flung out into space and whirled round and round together with oars and tubs and spars and gear of every sort.

Then he struck the water and went deep into it. Clawing his way upward he collided with the underside of a whale. Hal's breath had already been knocked out of him and if he could not get to the surface very soon he would drown.

Which way should he go? He should try to come out on the flank, but he could not tell how the whale lay. If by mistake he went towards the rear a whip of the tail might knock him senseless. If he went forward it would be an even greater mistake.

He swam, his back brushing against the whale's hide. He kept groping for a flipper. If he found one he would know that he was on the whale's flank and could come up to breathe.

Presently his hand grasped something that might be a flipper. He was about to pull himself up when he realized that this was no flipper — it was the edge of the whale's lower jaw. He was practically inviting himself to dinner. One snap of that great mouth and Hal Hunt would go to join his ancestors.

He backed off at once and came up at the whale's right side behind the fin. He had never thought to see the boat again, but there it was right-side up. It had landed luckily and had very little water in it. Oars and gear floated all about. Hal, after a deep breath or two to replenish his starved lungs, joined with the other men in collecting the floating articles, chucking them back into the boat and climbing in after them. Third mate Brown counted heads. Not a man was missing.

'All right, boys,' said Brown, raising his voice to be heard above the spouts and splashes of the whales. 'You're lucky to be alive. Oars! Let's get out of here.'

'Easier said than done!' growled Bruiser.

The boat rammed head-on into a whale.

'Try backing up,' commanded the third mate.

A few strokes backward and the way was blocked by an uncle.

The boat was trapped in whales. It lay in a bit of water no bigger than a swimming-pool, with whales all round it. They closed in upon it. The big bull,

smarting from his wound, began to rush off across the sea, and all the others with him. The whole pod moved like one animal, and snugly packed in the centre was the whale-boat, in peril of being crushed at any moment between the great flanks.

And yet even at such a time a whaleman thinks of barrels of oil. Brown seized the lance and went forward. The boat was snugged up tightly to the side of the big bull. It was a perfect set-up for a killing. A perfect chance for Brown to kill the whale, an equally perfect chance that the whale and his pals would kill every man aboard.

Brown stood in the bow with lance raised. He was enveloped in spray thrown up by the speeding boat and thrown down by the spouting whales. He looked like a statue in a fountain.

The lance went home. Deep, deep it went, and the whale in one convulsive movement struck the water with its head and tail, raising its middle so that it looked like a great black arch over the waves.

'Back away!' yelled Brown.

But there was no room to back away. The eighty-foot arch came down with a thunderous crash, barely missing the boat. The wave produced by the fall of some one hundred and twenty tons of whale washed the boat high up on to the flank of an uncle, from which it slid back into the sea, still right side up but full of water to the gunwales.

The men bailed furiously, expecting another attack at any moment. But they looked up to see with astonishment that the big whale had left them. It was swimming away from the pod.

The reason was plain. The ship had drawn nearer, and the great whale in its agony was about to attack it.

If that rock-hard head collided squarely with the keel below the water-line the timbers would be stove in. Many a sailing ship had been sunk in this fashion, and occasionally a vessel under steam power or diesel.

Grindle in the rings could be heard bawling orders to the helmsman. The ship began to veer to port. The whale was ploughing ahead at a good twenty knots. The men watched anxiously. Would the ship turn in time?

Whale and ship met. Men breathed again. It had not been a square hit. The whale struck the vessel's side a glancing blow and slid off towards the stern. The vessel shook itself like a dog and the sails shivered, but her hull was still sound beneath her.

The whale did not try again. He seemed to remember that he had some unfinished business to attend to. Back he came towards the boat, whose deadly irons were already draining away his life. He was still spouting, but now his spout blazed blood-red.

'His chimney's afire!' yelled one of the men.

The monster sank out of sight.

'He's done for!' shouted one.

'No such luck!' came the voice of the second mate whose boat was still held off by the circling uncle. He called to Brown:

'Look out below!'

'Aye aye, sir!'

Brown and his crew looked over the gunwales

into the depths. Hal at first could see nothing. Then he made out a small white spot. It seemed only as big as a hand, but it was rising and it rapidly grew in size as it rose.

Then he could make it out plainly. It was the open mouth of the bull whale. The enormous teeth, each as big as Hal's head, were ready for action.

'Full astern!' yelled Brown.

The men pulled, but it was no use. A whale blocked the way, and there was another ahead. With terrible speed the open jaws rose towards the middle of the boat. The men tumbled out of the way, some aft, some forward.

One man was not quick enough. He was caught between the two twenty-foot jaws as they closed in, one on either side of the boat, and crushed it like an eggshell.

The two ends of the crippled craft drifted apart, men in the water clinging to them, and thanking their stars they had something to cling to.

What had happened to the man who had been caught? There was just a chance that he lay unharmed in the beast's mouth and would be thrown out when the jaws opened. Hal watched anxiously.

But when the great mouth sprang open it was empty. The monster that could attack and devour a cuttle-fish almost as large as itself had had no difficulty in swallowing this human morsel.

If the man had escaped being injured by the closing teeth, was he still alive? It was a fantastic thought. However, there was the story of Jonah and the whale, a story that was supposed to be based upon fact. The stomach of a whale was as big as a good-sized cupboard. There might possibly be enough air in it to sustain life for a short time. Now and then a shark, still alive, has been taken from a whale's stomach. But a man is not so tough as a shark.

The mad bull thrashed about among the wreckage, his great jaws crunching everything within reach. The men had to let go their hold upon the pieces of the boat and swim to one side. There was always the danger of an attack by the other whales. Sharks had been drawn by the smell of blood and Hal splashed vigorously to keep them off.

He yelled a warning to one of his companions as he saw a shark about to seize his foot. The man, numbed by fear and cold, did not act in time. The razor teeth closed on his leg and he was drawn down.

Hal at once dived down in the hope of rescuing him. He explored the blue depths in vain. There were plenty of sharks about, but no sign of the man and the shark that had taken him.

He battled his way back through the gleaming silver bodies to the surface and came up by the rolling flank of the big whale.

13
Wild Ride

His hand struck something hard and cold. It was the harpoon in the whale's neck. Instinctively he grasped it and felt himself lifted out of the water and carried away at high speed.

The bull, having destroyed the boat, had now changed his tactics and was trying to run from the pain that tormented him. The rest of the pod followed at a slower pace. Sharks snapped alongside and Hal drew his feet up out of their way. He was thankful to the big bull. The monster that he had been helping to kill was now saving him.

He looked back and saw with relief that the two other boats were now able to come in and pick up the survivors.

Would anyone think about him? Some of them must have seen him dive, but perhaps no one had seen him rise again, because he had come up on the off side of the whale. They could not know what a wild ride he was getting.

Many a man had ridden horseback, camel-back, elephant-back and even ostrich-back, but who had ever gone for a ride whaleback?

In other circumstances he might have thought it

was great sport. It was like riding on the bridge of a submarine before it submerges.

Submerges. That was an unhappy thought. If this living submarine took a notion to dive, what would happen to its rider?

The bull, as if the same idea had just occurred to him, slid below the surface. Hal caught his breath as his head went under, and held on grimly. Perhaps this was just a surface dive. On the other hand it might be a 'sound', a dive far down to a depth of as much as a quarter of a mile. The whale might stay down for an hour. Three minutes of that would be quite enough to exhaust Hal's air, and the terrific pressure would crush him as flat and dead as a pancake.

But he had no sooner thought of these things than his head rose again above the waves. The whale sent up a terrific spout of blood and steam. And Hal remembered being told that a whale spouting blood never sounds, perhaps because its pierced lungs and drained arteries cannot retain enough oxygen for a long stay under water. However this may be, the big bull made only brief dips below water, coming up within a minute or so.

Every time he emerged he blasted more blood into the air which showered down upon Hal until he was so plastered from head to toe that his own mother would not have known him.

Wherever this deposit touched his skin it stung like fire. It was not the blood that caused this violent irritation, but the poison gases expelled from the monster's lungs. The wind blew these vapours back upon Hal along with the blood.

During a whale's stay of a half hour or an hour beneath the sea the pure air with which it has filled its lungs gradually changes, much as it does in the human body. Perhaps if a human could bottle up his breath for a half-hour or an hour it would, when expelled, be poisonous too.

The whale's spout is not kind to any living thing that gets in its way. A sailor who looked over the gunwale of his ship just as a whale below happened to spout got the blast full in his face; the skin itched terribly and a day later peeled off so that he looked as if he had come through a fire. Fortunately his eyes had automatically closed when the jet struck him. Eyes fully exposed to the fumes may be seriously damaged or even blinded.

If the healthy whale's spout is poisonous, the breath of a wounded whale is much more so. Again, the whale is like you and me. When we are sick or suffering or badly worried, the breath is not apt to be as sweet as when we are healthy and happy.

Hal, feeling the smart on his skin, was learning the hard way about the breathing of a whale and prudently closed his eyes whenever it spouted.

He looked back anxiously. No one was coming to his rescue. The two surviving boats had gone back to the ship. His mad race had covered more than a mile and every moment he was being carried farther and farther away.

Should he slide off into the sea and try to swim back? He would never make it. The water was alive with sharks. On both sides of the blood-spouting whale their long silver bodies flashed through the water as they kept up with the monster that they hoped soon to devour. The picture of the seaman hauled down by the shark was still fresh in Hal's mind. He had no desire to go to Davy Jones's locker by that route. His only chance was to hang on, and hope.

Would this great bull ever give up? He still ploughed along like a speed-boat. As the distance lengthened the ship gradually sank below the horizon. Now the hull was gone, the deck had disappeared. He could still see the masts, but they were steadily growing shorter.

He strained his eyes, hoping to see someone at the masthead. There was no look-out in the rings. Captain Grindle had gone down when the whale had attacked the ship.

Probably right now, thought Hal, they're holding a funeral service for those two poor fellows.

He was almost right. A funeral service was being held, but it was for three poor fellows, not two. Hal was counted among the dead. Roger was roused from his bunk to hear the sad news.

'Sorry, kid,' said third mate Brown. 'Your brother dived to help a chum who had just been pulled down by a shark. That's the last we saw of either of them.'

'But you don't really know that he died,' Roger insisted.

'Look, kid,' Brown explained patiently, 'when a man goes down and doesn't come up, there's only one answer. The boats that came in to pick us up — they rowed all over the place to make sure they weren't missing anybody. No use fooling yourself.

The sharks got him. We looked everywhere. You can trust us. We know our business.'

'But you don't know my brother. He's met sharks before and he didn't let them take him. I'll bet he's alive. Couldn't we go out and look again?'

'It ain't no use,' said Brown. 'But if you want to ask the Captain — '

Roger at once went to Captain Grindle.

'Captain, may we take out a boat and look for my brother?'

The captain looked as indignant as if he had been asked to send a boat to the moon.

'You impudent young squirt, what do you think we are? Do you suppose we have nothing to do but hunt for gents who don't know enough to take care of themselves?'

'But that's just it,' said Roger. 'He does know how to take care of himself. That's why I feel he's still alive.'

'And where d'you suppose he'd be?' sneered Grindle. 'In a mermaid's palace at the bottom of the sea, I suppose. He wasn't afloat, or he woulda sung out when the boats went looking. Or perhaps you think he got flung so high in the air that he hasn't come down yet.' He grinned his evil sarcastic grin, then turned harsh again. 'We've done all we can for your fool brother. We gave him a nice funeral service, some pretty words from Holy Scriptures, and a watery grave. Your brother just wasn't tough enough for this life. It should be a lesson to all gents who think they're real he-men.'

He gripped Roger by the shoulder and brought

his porcupine beard uncomfortably close to the boy's face.

'And if you really want to know what I think happened to your brother, I'll tell you. He knew he was going to be flogged within an inch of his life if he came back to this ship. That put him in a funk. When a man is scared he can't defend himself. Your brother was scared and the sharks got him.'

14
Alone

In the meantime, Hal, very much alive, was beginning to face the possibility that he would not be alive much longer.

The whale was steadily losing blood. In due time it must roll over, 'fin out', as whalers say when a whale dies. Then the sharks would close in and make a dinner on the carcass, with Hal as dessert.

Even if the whale lived the prospect was not bright. It would plough on far away into unknown seas. Its rider would bake in the heat of the tropical sun by day and, always wet to the skin, would shiver in the cold night wind that sweeps across the ocean after dark even on the Equator. He would endure the agonies of hunger and thirst until his mind would fail, his grip on the iron would loosen and he would slip off into the sea.

The masts of the *Killer* had disappeared. There was nothing to be seen but a million humping waves. He felt terribly alone.

Then he remembered that he was not alone. Beneath him, inside this animal submarine, there was another human being.

Suppose this modern Jonah was alive. What

dreadful thoughts he must be having as he found himself imprisoned in this living tomb.

Was he fighting to get out? If he could escape from the stomach through the gullet into the mouth, what were his chances? The muscles of swallowing would force him back into his prison. Or he would be crushed by the huge teeth. At the very best he might slip out of the mouth whenever it opened, but then he would only be the helpless prey of the sharks.

More likely there was no breath of life left in him, and Hal was truly alone.

He was startled to hear a deep groan.

Had he really heard it, or was his own mind beginning to give way? Then it came again, a sad and painful sound. He realized that the mournful voice he heard was the voice of the suffering whale beneath him.

He felt at that moment that he would never want to kill another whale.

Hal was not merely imagining that he heard the voice of the whale. Whales are not dumb. They have no vocal chords, yet they make a great variety of sounds. Some naturalists believe that whales 'talk', or at least signal to each other by means of sounds. The Woods Hole Oceanographic Institution has recorded the sounds by tape recorder. The zoologist Ivan T. Sanderson says in *Follow the Whale*: 'It is now known that all whales, and especially porpoises and some dolphins, keep up a tremendous racket underwater, lowing like cows, moaning, whistling, and making chuckling sounds . . . Belugas have an enormous vocabulary of different sounds, which gives rise to their popular name among seamen of "sea canaries". They twitter, whistle, scream, gurgle, chuckle, hoot, and make strange popping and puffing noises.'

And it is not surprising that the whale has a voice. After all, it is not a fish, but a mammal like a cat or dog or the reader of this book.

Some millions of years ago it had four legs and waddled about on land. Perhaps it could not get enough to eat on shore to fill its great body and took to swimming after food. It became more and more used to the water, and after thousands of years its useless legs dwindled away.

The remains of them are still there. The front legs have changed into flippers, but inside each flipper may be found five toes left over from the time when whales walked the earth. And deep in the rear part of the whale are two useless bones, the remains of what were once hind legs.

So, thought Hal, this fellow is my cousin.

It helped a little. He did not feel quite so lost

and lonely in this watery waste when he remembered that the creature below him was, like himself, warm-blooded, breathed air, had a skeleton, brain, heart and blood vessels much like his own, and could feel pain, grief or joy as he could.

15
How to Steer a Whale

The big bull frequently changed direction. When south did not get him away from his misery he tried west, then east. If only he would head back towards the ship!

Hal wondered if there was any way to steer a whale. The whale is one of the most intelligent of beasts. Hal had seen, on his father's animal farm, how less intelligent animals than the whale could be guided here and there.

A horse even without a bridle could be steered by pressure of the rider's knees. A camel could be turned to the right or left by the rider's bare toes tickling his neck on one side or the other. The mahout on an elephant's back could make this mountain of flesh go to one side or the other by touching one of the big ears with his pole. And Hal had seen a rhino mother push her young one along ahead of her and direct its course by pressing her horn against its withers on the left side or the right.

But how to apply this knowledge to the problem of steering a whale was quite beyond him. Perhaps if he pulled out the lance and used it to stab one of the whale's ten-foot cheeks it would turn the other way.

It was not a bad idea and quite possibly it might have worked — but Hal couldn't do it. The big bull had become a person to him, almost a friend. He could not add to its suffering.

'The Cap is right,' he said to himself. 'I'm a softie.'

Hal still held on to the harpoon with one hand. His other hand held the rope which trailed away from the harpoon back over the waves, its end having been torn loose from the broken boat.

Could he use this rope? The idea appealed to his sense of humour. He laughed aloud at the notion of putting a bridle on a whale. His laugh frightened himself, it seemed so out of place in this desolate silence.

Well, anyhow, he could try it. He gathered up several fathoms of the line, looped it as he had so often done for lassoing animals on the farm, and threw it twenty feet forward so that the bight dropped just beyond the animal's head and was drawn tight at the mouth. Hal held two reins in his hands. He felt like Neptune, lord of the sea, driving his chariot over the waves.

According to the sun, he calculated that the ship was a little east of north. He must pull on the right rein. As he began to do so the bull, annoyed by this thing like the tentacle of an octopus that rubbed across his lips, opened his jaws and took the line firmly in his teeth.

Hal pulled manfully on the right rein. It might have worked on a one-ton horse, or even on a seven-ton elephant. It had no effect whatever on the one-hundred-and-twenty-ton bull of the sea.

No effect except to annoy still more the whale which now savagely bit the rope in two. Hal hauled in the rope and looked at the place where it had been cut apart as if with a knife. He had had no idea that a whale's teeth could be so sharp.

All right, that was no good. But Hal's inventive mind did not give up. He must try, and keep on trying — his life depended upon it. What else could he do?

He might entangle the left fin in the rope so that it could not work properly. He had once seen in the aquarium a fish with a disabled ventral fin. Because only one fin was working the fish tended to turn in one direction.

But a whale does not swim like a fish. A fish uses its fins as well as its tail to propel it through the water. The whale uses only its enormous twenty-foot-wide tail. The fins are used merely for balancing. Hal saw that they were quite motionless. He gave up the idea of lassoing a fin.

What else did a whale have that might influence his direction? It had ears.

Hanging on to the harpoon rope he slid down to one of the ears, very small for a brute of such size. He plugged the ear with rope and waited for results. There were none. The whale continued steadily in the same direction. Hal removed the rope from the ear.

But the eyes. Why hadn't he thought of them before?

A whale's eyes are planted in the sides of the

head, not the front. The whale can see nothing behind him and very little ahead. He sees to the left with the left eye and to the right with the right eye.

Like a bird, thought Hal. Or a horse.

He had once owned a horse named Right. He was called that because he always had a tendency to go to the right. He was blind in the left eye. Any animal likes to see where it is going, and since this horse could see right he went right.

It was always necessary for the driver to keep a tight left rein if he wished to go straight. A normal horse would continue straight even if the reins were dropped. Not so Right. As soon as the reins went slack he would begin to shy away slightly from the world he could not see and which might contain any number of dangers and edge over into the world that his good eye told him was safe.

The ocean, too, has its dangers. The sensible whale would want to avoid them — dangers such as rocks and shoals, schools of sharks or swordfish, the giant cuttle-fish with his horny beak, and men in boats. If the whale could see only to one side, his instinct for safety should cause him to favour that side.

Hal put his theory to the test. He stripped off his blood-caked shirt and let it hang from his hand so that its folds covered the whale's left eye.

The great bull seemed to take no notice. He had been going due west and he kept going due west. Hal persisted for a good five minutes, but there was no change.

Bitterly disappointed, he was about to haul up

his shirt when he happened to glance again at the sun. It was not quite where it had been. Yes, the whale was veering ever so slightly to the right. His direction was a shade north of west, then a definite west-north-west, then full north-west.

Hal was in an uncomfortable and dangerous position. Huddled part-way down the whale's left flank, he was hanging on to the harpoon rope with one hand and with the other operating his blinder. It was hard to block the whale's vision continually because gusts of wind kept blowing the shirt aside. Hal was so close to the water that the sharks took a great interest in him and frequently thrust their jaws above the surface in an effort to reach a leg or an arm.

But the whale was steadily edging towards what he could see and away from what he could not see. From north-west he slowly swung to north. When he had turned a few degrees east of north Hal was satisfied that his black chariot was now headed for the ship. He took away the blinder and climbed up the rope to the higher and safer point beside the harpoon.

But his work was not done. Every once in a while the bull would take a notion to charge off towards another point of the compass. Then Hal would have to slip down and cover sometimes the left eye, sometimes the right, to get his speed-boat back on course.

And wasn't the speed-boat slowing down? That was new cause for worry. The tips of the *Killer*'s masts were now above the horizon. But there was still a long way to go. The whale's enormous flukes beat less rapidly, his groans were more frequent, his spouts more thick with blood and only half as high as they had been. At any moment he might give up and roll over fin out, throwing his rider to the sharks.

Hal focused his tired and poisoned eyes upon the mastheads of the whaling ship. He thought he could make out a black blob near the head of the foremast. Soon he was sure, and his discouragement and fear gave way to new hope. There was a look-out in the foremast rings. Hal shouted for joy. His own voice frightened him, it was so quickly soaked up by the great silence.

Perhaps the look-out would not see the whale after all. The man at the masthead watches for a white spout, but the spout of this whale was a dull red and now so low that it would scarcely appear above the wave-tops. The whale's body might be seen, or it might not, for the dying bull was not swimming as high out of the water as before and his tiring flukes made no splash.

Hal could not see who was in the rings. He hoped it was a good man, one with keen eyes. Hal's fate depended upon those eyes.

The whale was weakening fast and the throb of his twenty-foot propeller almost stopped at times. Then with a savage grunt he would make a new spurt forward. These spurts became slower and shorter until at last the monster lay without motion, wallowing in the waves. As a last gesture of defiance, the great bull sent up a column of red mist into the sky.

16
Rescue

Hal thought he heard a cry across the sea. It might have been only the scream of a gull — but it might have been the call of the look-out. He listened intently. Now he heard it again and there was no mistake. It came faint but clear:

'Blows! Blows!'

Thank the Lord for the sharp eyes of that look-out, thought Hal. He had been seen. No, not he, but the whale. He himself would not be visible at that distance, especially since his colour was exactly the same as that of the whale's back, both painted dull red by the bloody spouts.

He saw another figure climb into the rings. That would be the captain. The look-out went down out of sight.

'Bless his hide, whoever he is,' said Hal fervently.

It seemed a very long time before the boats appeared. The men in those boats were coming after a whale — they could have no idea that a man was aboard.

Hal prepared to give them the surprise of their lives. He lay flat on the far side so that he could not be seen by the men in the approaching boats.

What a pleasure it was to hear human voices once again, so much more cheering than the groan of a perishing whale.

'All right. Pull up alongside.' It was the voice of the second mate. 'What in Heaven's name do we have here? Look, he has a harpoon in him! And a lance! I'm staggered if it isn't that same old bull — the one that gave us all that trouble and then ran out on us.'

Other voices chimed in.

'Whatever brought him back!'

'Perhaps he came back to do us in. Look out for him!'

'No, he's done for. He'll roll over any minute.'

Hal thought it was time to make his appearance. He crawled up so that just his head showed above the whale's back.

'Am I seeing things?' cried someone. 'What's that?'

They might well be puzzled. Hal's face and head were caked over with half-dried blood.

Hal stood up, red from head to foot.

The men stared in disbelief.

'It's the divvil himself,' muttered one, crossing himself.

'It's Hal!' cried Roger leaping to his feet. Hal grinned a bloody but happy grin to see his brother whom he had almost feared he would never set eyes on again.

He slid down into the nearest boat. At once he was bombarded with questions.

'Where you been?'

'We saw you dive but you didn't come up. What happened?'

'How far did he take you?'

'How did you get so stinkin' bloody?'

The questions were interrupted by the big bull. Irritated by the presence of the boats, he turned to attack them. He opened his great boatsize jaws. But he was not his old self. His movements were sluggish, and the oarsmen easily pulled their craft out of his way.

The huge jaws came together with a thunderous crash. The bull sent up a last brave spout that fluttered like a red banner in the wind. A low groan came from the depths of him and he rolled over, belly up.

'Throw a line over that tail,' ordered the mate, 'and we'll tow him to the ship.'

'Wait a minute,' said Hal. 'First we'd better try to save the other chap.'

'What other? Were there two of you?'

'Yes.'

The men looked at each other understandingly. Hal's terrifying experience must have affected his mind.

'Try to calm down,' the second mate said. 'There isn't any other.'

'I don't have time to explain,' Hal said, snatching a knife. 'If we're quick we may get him out alive.'

Avoiding the men who tried to stop him, he leaped out on to the dead whale's white belly. He began to make a lengthwise cut over the region of the stomach. The men looked on in astonishment, wagging their heads.

'Crazy as a loon,' one said.

The skin on a whale's underside is more tender than elsewhere. Hal had soon made an opening eight feet long. If the men wanted any further proof that he was crazy, they got it when he dropped through the opening into the stomach of the whale.

He found himself in a chamber some fourteen feet long and five across, lit only by the light coming through the slit above. He felt the sting of gastric juices on his face and his bare trunk.

He wondered if anybody had ever before gone inside a whale. Probably. In Africa when an elephant is killed the hungry men go inside to get the heart, kidneys and other choice portions of meat. And there is much more room in a whale than in an elephant.

Groping about, his hand struck something that might be the horny beak of a cuttle-fish. Then he found his companion. He lifted him so that his head emerged from the slit along with his own.

When the men in the boats saw this strange sight they could well believe it was not Hal who had gone crazy, but they themselves. Their amazement grew when Hal climbed out, and pulled the other man out after him.

Now several men leaped up beside him and willing hands eased the still form down into the boat.

The mate tested for respiration and heartbeat. Hal hoped desperately. If a shark had been brought out alive from the stomach of a whale, why not a man? The mate finished his examination, and shook his head.

'It was a bit too much for him.'

Two men had paid for this whale with their lives. The high cost of cold cream, Hal thought. Whale oil was used to make cold cream as well as many other useful products. But did the young woman who sat before a mirror applying cosmetics to her face realize what they had cost — not in money, but in struggle, strain and life itself? Did the person washing his hands with soap containing whale oil realize what it had cost to put it in his hands? The users of glycerine, margarine, paints, varnishes, textiles, fertilizer, cattle fodder, vitamins made with whale-liver oil, hormones obtained from the glands of the whale, many life-saving drugs, gifts from the whale to man — did the people who made daily use of these things ever think of the men who had fought and died to provide them?

Not to mention the monarch of the sea that had perished so that his human cousins might be a little more healthy and happy.

The line was out over the tail and the long job of towing the monster back to the ship began. Meanwhile the questions continued.

Hal told how he had steered the great whale.

'Now you're spoofing us,' said one man. 'Steer a whale, my grandmother!'

But the other men were inclined to believe Hal. After all, there was the whale. Durkins turned to the expert on whales, Mr Scott. 'What does the professor say?'

'Hal was lucky enough or smart enough,' Scott

said, 'to hit on something that has been known to zoologists for a long time — that any animal with eyes in the sides of its head instead of in front will tend to favour the side with better vision. It's a scientific fact. More than that, it's just common sense. You take more interest in what you can see than what you can't. Suppose you had eyes in the back of your head instead of in front. Would you want to walk forward?'

'No, backward,' said Durkins.

'Right. And it's the same way with the whale. If his view is cut off to one side, he'll edge over to the other. But not everybody would have thought of it. I think you owe Hunt your thanks for bringing home a fine whale.'

'Bet your life!' agreed Durkins, and the rest of the men chimed in. They began to speculate on how many barrels of oil the monster would yield and how much extra pay it would mean for every man.

'But,' Hal said, 'the fellow you really ought to thank is that look-out. Without him, you wouldn't have had a whale. He must have been pretty sharp, because the whale was low in the water and wasn't spouting white.'

'Do you want to know who the look-out was?' asked Durkins.

'I certainly do.'

'He was your kid brother.'

Hal grinned at Roger and his heart was pretty full. There was a lot he wanted to say, but all he could say now was: 'Good job!'

'The kid wouldn't believe us when we told him

you were dead,' the mate went on. 'Guess he knew you were a hard nut to crack. He pestered the Captain till Grindle let him go up in the rings and watch.'

'I thought I might see you hanging on to a piece of wreckage somewhere,' Roger said. 'Then this whale came along. I didn't see you on its back but I had a sort of hunch you weren't far away.'

'You sure surprised us when you popped up over that whale's back,' Durkins said. 'I hope to see the Cap's face when his eyes light on you. He thinks you're at the bottom of the sea.'

A sudden shadow fell upon the boats. The men looked up to see that a dark grey mist had swallowed the sun. From the cloud-bank long tails of mist spiralled down to the sea.

'Fog!' said Durkins. 'In ten minutes we won't be able to see a thing. Pull, boys, while you can still see the ship.'

Heavy wet curtains of fog settled down until they brushed the wave-tops. Seen through the curtains, the ship came and went as if it was only a dream, not an actual vessel on a real ocean. The men looked uneasy. Sailors are superstitious, and to their minds the sea is never so mysterious as when veiled in fog. It is at such times that the Flying Dutchman is seen, or imagined. And such ghostly visions appear as those described by Coleridge in *The Rime of the Ancient Mariner.*

A sighing sound came from the heavens. Some of the men fingered charms that hung round their necks, and their lips moved as they repeated silently magical words that were supposed to fend off the evil eye. Now the ship was gone and the fog closed in like a smothering blanket over the boats.

The mate tried to pep up his men: 'It won't last long. Keep at it, boys. Only a cable's length to go.'

At one moment there was nothing ahead. At the next moment the boats were ramming their noses into the hull of the *Killer*. A man clambered up the ship's forechains with the whale's tow-line and made it fast. The boats were eased back to the rope ladder that rose to the deck.

The fog was so heavy that the men in the boats could not see Captain Grindle at the top of the ladder, nor could the captain see them. But he could hear their voices and the clugging of the oars in the oarlocks.

'Ahoy, down there!' called the captain.

It was the second mate who should have called back. Instead, he put his finger to his lips, signalling his men to be quiet. Then he whispered to Hal:

'Let's give the old geezer the scare of his life. You go up alone. I'll bet he'll think you're a zombie.'

17
The Ghost in the Fog

Hal climbed the rope ladder. He tried to move without making a sound. He raised his face and saw Captain Grindle looking down. The captain's eyes were great balls of terror. He tried to speak, but could not. He backed away from the rail as Hal rose before him.

The fog-blinded captain could see very little and could not believe what he saw. This thing, plastered with red from head to foot, looked more like a demon than a man. It reminded Grindle of the Gent. But it could not be. The Gent was drowned and a funeral service had been said over him.

This vision, appearing and disappearing through the fog, must be his ghost. It had come back to take revenge. The captain suddenly regretted that he had ever insulted the Gent or threatened him with a flogging.

Hal stood up on the gunwhale. His burning eyes looking out from the mask of blood terrified the captain. Grindle backed away, muttering: 'No, no!' And again: 'No, no! Don't.'

The other men were now climbing to the deck to see the fun. Hal spread his arms as if he were about to take off from his perch on the gunwhale and fly at his enemy. The captain, still backing up, stumbled against the rim of a pan of porridge that the cook had put out to cool and sat down in it, splashing the pasty stuff in all directions.

He was up again in a hurry and retreated to the companionway that led down to his cabin.

At this distance he felt safer and began to bluster.

'You, whoever you are, get down off that rail. If you don't, I'll shoot you down.' He began to reach back for his revolver.

Before he could touch it, Hal was swinging towards him at the end of a clew-line from the mainsail yard-arm. The fog hid the line. All the captain could see was an indistinct something flying straight towards him through mid-air like an angel of Satan.

With a bellow of fear he started down the companionway, lost his footing, tumbled and bumped all the way to the bottom, scrambled into his cabin and locked the door.

He lay trembling in his bunk, fearfully watching the door. A phantom that could float through the air could certainly come through a locked door. Or through a porthole. One of the portholes was open and he crawled over to close it, but before he could do so he heard a strange sound.

Roars of laughter drifted down from the deck. All his men were screaming with joy. What was so funny? He listened to catch any words. He heard shouts of: 'Good boy, Hunt!' 'You gave him a proper fright.' 'That will teach the old bully.' 'Three cheers for Hunt!'

125

The captain stopped trembling. He wiped the sweat from his forehead and a cold rage crept over him.

So they were laughing at him. The thing he had seen was not a ghost, it was Hunt himself. But how could that be? He had buried Hunt and logged him as dead. The log-book lay open on the desk and there was the entry:

> Seaman Hal Hunt, losing his life through his own carelessness and stupidity, was this day consigned to the sea with all due rites of funeral, though undeserving of such honour.

There it was. He was dead and gone and buried, but he was alive and on deck at this very moment. There should be a law against this sort of thing. A man once logged dead had no right to come back. It was a breach of discipline and ought to be punished.

The captain had so enjoyed writing that item in that log — now he regretfully crossed it out. This spoiled the appearance of the page: that was Hal's fault and he would have to suffer for it. The captain was now boiling with resentment and injured pride. They would laugh at him, would they? Well, he would have the last laugh.

He took out his revolver and made sure that every chamber was full. He was the only man on board with a gun. That thought made him swell up with importance. It did not occur to him that only a coward would use a gun against unarmed men.

Thanks to his gun he could command obedience.

He would make an example of this Hunt, such a terrible example that no man on board would ever forget it. This fellow must be flogged within an inch of his life. Forty strokes of the cat was the usual punishment on the *Killer* — this time it would be eighty. With what pleasure he would write it down in his log!

Why not write it now? Then he would be bound to carry it through. Nothing could stop him. He would have to do it because it was already written. He wrote:

On this day, Seaman Hal Hunt, guilty of defying established authority, received eighty lashes.

There it was, in black and white, and this time he would not have to cross it out. It was going to be done, and at once.

Gritting his teeth on this resolve the captain unlocked the door and went up the companionway, gun in hand. At the top, he peered round the doorjamb to see what was going on.

The men were marching round the deck carrying Hal Hunt on their shoulders. They were laughing, cheering, shouting: 'Hooray for Hunt!'

With a grim smile on his porcupine face, Captain Grindle aimed his revolver just above the head of the man who had returned from the grave.

He fired. The bullet whizzed above the crew and thudded into the mainmast. The men stopped cheering. Hal was dropped to the deck. Some of the men ran to the fo'c'sle. Others hid behind the masts.

127

Captain Grindle, much pleased with the effect of his shot, strode out on to the deck. He was every inch the master, and he gloried in the feeling.

'Bruiser!' he bawled. 'Come forward!'

The ex-prizefighter stepped out, cringing like a small boy. 'I didn't do anything, sir,' he said, his eye on the captain's gun.

'Spread-eagle that man!'

'What man?'

'The Gent.'

An angry murmur ran through the crowd. Bruiser stood irresolute. Second mate Durkins cast about for a way to gain time.

'Begging your pardon, sir,' he said, 'the man the whale got — his body is in the boat. Shouldn't we give him a funeral first?'

'He's already had his funeral. Tell Sails to stitch him up in a piece of canvas and dump him overboard.'

The man nicknamed Sails because it was his job to look after the ship's canvas, retired to perform this unhappy duty.

The captain would not let himself be side-tracked from his purpose. 'Bruiser, did you hear my order?'

The second mate tried again.

'Sir, this man Hunt has given us a big whale. It's well over a hundred barrels, sir. He brought it back single-handed.'

The captain flew into a rage. He fired twice and men dropped to the deck to get out of the way of the singing bullets.

'What!' he cried. 'Am I to be questioned and

128

corrected by my own officers? The next time I fire it won't be for fun. And you,' he pointed the gun at Bruiser, 'will be my target if you don't carry out my orders. Spread-eagle the Gent!'

Bruiser still hesitated, and the captain might have carried out his threat if Hal had not stepped forward.

'Better do as he says,' Hal said, and placed himself with his face against the mainmast and his arms stretched forward around the mast, his legs braced apart. Bruiser bound the two hands together, thus tightly securing the victim to the mast. From a utility chest the captain pulled out the cat-o'-nine-tails and put it in Bruiser's hand.

'Eighty lashes!' he ordered.

Again an angry growl went through the crew. Then Scott, the scientist, pushed his way through the crowd and faced Captain Grindle.

'Captain, may I have a word with you — in private?'

'Can't it wait till this is done?'

'I'm afraid not,' said Scott. Placing his hand on the captain's arm he led him back out of earshot.

'Captain, I am a passenger on this ship and not one of your crew, so you may allow me to speak to you frankly. I would earnestly advise you not to flog this man. Flogging belongs to the old days — it is forbidden by modern maritime law.'

'Now let me tell you something,' said the angry captain. 'This ship belongs to the old days. So do I. I've always made my own law aboard ship and I intend to keep right on making it. If that's all you have to say to me, you're wasting your time.'

'It's not quite all,' said Scott, trying to keep his voice polite and reasonable. 'Hunt may have been impertinent — but I think you might excuse him since he has just done you a very great service.'

'Done me a great service? How?'

'By bringing in this whale. It was really a very remarkable feat. The whale, as you well know, is worth round about three thousand pounds, and a good proportion of the profit goes to you. The rest will be divided among the men. Naturally they are very happy about it and Hunt is very popular with them. If you have him flogged, I don't think they'll stand for it.'

The captain's face behind the black bristles flushed an angry red. 'You threaten me with mutiny? Do you know I could clap you in irons for that? You're a passenger, but remember I'm master over passengers as well as crew. You'll do well to keep a civil tongue in your head.'

'I'm trying to keep a civil tongue,' said Scott. What else could he say to influence this stubborn bully? He would try flattery. 'I know you're the master, and I know you're a strong man and I know that even without a gun you're the equal of any man on board.'

'Equal?' snapped the captain. 'I'm better. There's not a man in the crew who could stand up to me in a fair fight.'

'Not even Hunt?'

The captain fell into the trap.

'Hunt? Why, I could take him apart with my bare hands.'

'Now you're talking!' exclaimed Scott, pretending to be lost in admiration. 'That sounds like a real man. No gun. A man like you doesn't need a gun. You could leave it in your cabin. You wouldn't be afraid to do that. Not you.'

'Afraid?' scoffed Grindle. 'I'll show you how afraid I am of that young squirt.'

He took out the revolver and went down the companionway to his cabin. He came back without the gun. He strode up the deck to the mainmast.

18
Grindle Takes a Blubber Bath

'Loose that man,' he ordered.

Bruiser, wonderingly, unbound Hal's hands. Hal turned about to face the captain.

Grindle's pop eyes swept haughtily over his crew like a pair of searchlights.

'Breach of discipline,' he said, 'don't go on the *Killer*. It has to be punished. Yesterday this man made insulting remarks about my ability to run a ship. Today he has the impudence to come back from the dead and try to scare me with a pack o' ghost tricks. He didn't scare me a bit. I'm so little scared of him I'm going to give him a choice. A choice between the cat and these two hands!'

He stopped for a moment to let the idea soak in.

'It ain't fair,' came a voice from the crowd. 'You got a gun.'

'No gun,' said Grindle. 'It's below decks. A man like me don't need a gun. The science fellow says so, and he's right. Don't need a cat neither. Just my own bare hands, that's enough. And when I get done with this varmint he won't have one bone connected to another.'

He turned to Hal. 'Or perhaps you'd rather have the eighty? Whichever you prefer. Our aim is to oblige.' He bowed in mock courtesy.

It was not easy for Hal to decide. Eighty lashes would, he knew, leave him an unconscious bleeding heap on the deck. Men had died under the blows of the cat-o'-nine-tails. The alternative was a hand-to-hand fight with Grindle. That could be tough too. Hal was tall and powerful for his age, but Grindle was enough taller so that he could look straight over Hal's head. He was heavier and more solidly set. Long years of sea life had put muscles that bulged like sausages under the skin of his arms and back of his shoulder-blades. His hands were as big as meat-hooks.

'Come on, Gent!' demanded Grindle. 'Cat or hands?'

'Hands,' said Hal and closed with his opponent. At once he felt the hands that he had invited locked round his own throat. Hal ducked and plunged his head into the big fellow's stomach. Grindle let out a grunt of surprise and relaxed his grip just enough so that Hal could tear loose.

Hal backed off a few feet.

'Hah!' exclaimed Grindle. 'Running away already!'

He came fast, his big gorilla-like hands out-stretched.

Hal let him come. He even helped him to come. He seized one of the hands and pulled, twisting to the right at the same time. The captain went over

Hal's shoulder, turned a somersault and came down on his back on the deck. The breath was knocked out of him, and some of the conceit too.

Hal had not visited Japan in vain. While there, his Japanese friends had taught him some of the moves of judo (ju-jitsu). The principle of judo is to let your opponent destroy himself. You conquer by yielding. If he plunges at you you let him come, but step out of the way at the last moment and let him plunge into the wall. If he comes running you may trip him and give him a bad fall. His own speed is his undoing. If he swings a fist at you you may seize him by the wrist and increase his swing so that he throws his shoulder out of joint. If he exerts a nerve or muscle you may increase the strain to the danger-point by striking that nerve or muscle. At such a moment of strain, a slight tap on a sensitive spot may have a crippling effect. The judo-fighter is taught the location of these sensitive spots; for example the elbow, or funny bone, where a nerve is partially exposed, the armpit, the ankle, the wrist-bones, the liver, a tendon below the ear, the nerves of the upper arm and the Adam's apple.

In judo the man with the big muscles may be beaten by the man with the quick brain. Hal was no expert in judo, but he knew more about it than his opponent. His might not be as strong as the captain, but he was wiry, swift and intelligent. If Grindle was a lion, Hal was a panther.

The captain never knew where to find him. He lowered his head and charged like a bull, hoping to strike Hal in the solar plexus — he found himself butting the capstan instead. He shot his great fist towards Hal's face, but Hal moved his head to one side and the fist caught Bruiser an ugly crack on the jaw.

'Look out what you're doing,' growled Bruiser.

The men were laughing. The captain got the painful impression that he was making a fool of himself. Was he going to be beaten by this gent? Not if he knew it. He would bash the fellow's head in. He seized a belaying-pin.

'Not fair,' yelled the crowd. 'Hands only.'

Grindle swung the heavy club, but at the moment when it should have made contact with Hal's head he felt a sharp rap on his wrist that spoiled his grip and the weapon went overboard.

With a savage curse he pulled a knife from his belt. His crew booed him but he paid them no heed. He rushed at Hal, who retreated swiftly until he backed up against one of the try-pots. Grindle came on at a dead run. At the last moment Hal ducked, seized one of the captain's ankles and heaved. Grindle was lifted in the air and came down head-first into the pot.

Luckily for him the blubber was not boiling. The try-pots had been neglected when the big whale came in and the fire had burned low. The contents of the pot were like a rank-smelling jelly or paste, and when the captain's head finally popped up out of the mess it was completely covered with half-solid blubber. The men rocked with laughter.

The captain rubbed blubber from his eyes and spat blubber from his mouth. 'Get me out of here!' he screamed.

Hal and Bruiser pulled him out and he collapsed

on the deck in a puddle of grease. He still held his knife, but all the fight had gone out of him.

He stood up, dripping blobs of fat. He wobbled aft to his cabin and left a river of blubber behind him.

After he had stripped, cleaned himself as well as he could and put on fresh clothes, he sat down heavily to think things over. Before him on his desk was his open log-book. His eyes fell on the entry:

On this day, Seaman Hal Hunt, guilty of defying established authority, received eighty lashes.

He crossed it out.

19
Grindle Shakes Hands

Grindle took up his revolver.

He balanced it on the palm of his hand. This gun was his only friend. It felt good. Courage flowed from it up his arm and into his chest.

Much of the conceit had been cooked out of him by his plunge into the pot of whale grease. The gun made him feel better. He was still master, so long as he possessed the only firearm on the ship.

He could hear them still laughing on deck. His friend, the gun, would stop that. A gun has no sense of humour.

'I'll show them,' he muttered.

His anger grew as he looked at the spoiled page of his log. What would the ship's owners think when they read this page? A man was logged as dead, but wasn't dead. The same man got eighty lashes, but didn't. What kind of nonsense was this? The owners would think the captain a fool for writing such things and then crossing them out. Didn't he know his own mind?

He knew what he was going to do now, but he wouldn't write it down this time until it was done. As soon as he felt a little less wobbly he was going to go on deck with this gun and fill the Gent's carcass with bullets. Then he would write in his log that he had been compelled to use the gun in self-defence against an unruly seaman who had tried to murder him.

He thought this over. He began to see that it would not work. The crew was against him. If he shot Hunt they would report it to the police as soon as the ship reached port.

A sly grin came over his bristly face.

I've got it, he thought. I'll fool 'em. Make 'em think it's all right between me and the Gent. Pretend we let bygones be bygones. No hard feelings. We had a fight and it's all over and now we're as friendly as two kittens in a basket. And after I get them thinking that way they won't blame me when the Gent has an accident.

He settled back happily into his chair. A real bad accident. I'll fix it for him so he won't come out of it alive. But nobody'll be able to pin anything on me.

He got up and tried his legs. They still felt like two ribbons of spaghetti. His back was bruised where it had thumped the deck, his solar plexus ached where Hal had dived into it, and his head was battered where he had bashed it against the capstan.

He looked in the mirror. His skin had been blistered here and there by the hot blubber. He could be thankful it had not been hotter. But he was not thankful — only possessed by a terrible hate and passion for revenge.

To think that a nineteen-year-old boy had done

all this to him! Wrathfully he blew his nose; blubber filled his handkerchief. He wiped the last traces of blubber from the corners of his eyes, and dug blubber out of his ears. Despite all his cleaning, he still smelled like a dead whale.

He went up on deck. The fires had been built up again and the blubber in the try-pots was boiling. The black smoke rising from the whale-scraps that were fed into the fire, and the white steam rising from the try-pots swirled and swooped through the rigging like great black and white birds. Men dumped chunks of blubber into the pots and other men drew off the oil into barrels. At the same time men out on the cutting-stage were beginning to peel off the hide of Hal's great whale. Everyone was in great good humour, still laughing at what had happened to the captain.

'There he is!' someone warned, and they all quit work to see what would happen. 'He'll be hopping mad,' said one. 'He'll probably shoot the place up,' said another, and looked for something to hide behind. 'He'll kill Hunt,' said someone else. 'I'd hate to be in Hunt's shoes now.' Another said: 'If he lays a hand on Hunt, we'll finish him.'

But the captain did not pull his gun and he did not seem to be in a rage. In fact there was something almost like a smile behind the porcupine bristles.

'Hunt,' he called. 'I have something to say to you.'

Hal stepped forward. He was as wary as a cat, and ready to move fast if the captain drew his gun. But Grindle only stretched out his hand.

'Put it there,' he said. 'Let's shake hands and forget it. Nobody can say I ain't a good sport. It was a fair fight and you beat me and that's that. Shake.'

Hal did not remind the captain that it was not a fair fight. Instead of fighting hand to hand as agreed, Grindle had taken up a belaying-pin and then a knife. No good sport would do that. But Hal was so grateful for Grindle's change of heart that he impulsively shook the hand of the captain of the *Killer.*

'It's very handsome of you to feel that way about it,' Hal said. 'I was afraid you might be sore.'

'Me, sore!' Grindle laughed. 'Boy, you don't know me. Sore? On the contrary, it's a pleasure to find I've a real man on my ship. To show you how I feel about you, I'm going to promote you. From now on you're master harpooner.'

'But I've never thrown a harpoon,' Hal protested.

'Listen, boy,' said the captain, thrusting his evil-smelling bristles among which bits of blubber still remained close to Hal's face, 'anybody who can throw me can throw a harpoon.' He laughed loudly at his own joke. 'Yes sir, you're a harpooner from now on. Shake again!'

Hal shook again, but a little uncomfortably. He had the slightest suspicion that the captain was putting on an act. But he brushed it aside, for he was always inclined to believe the best about others and perhaps even the brutal Grindle had a good streak in him.

During the next few days the captain was persistently kind to Hal. This was not easy. Inside the captain's barrel chest was a churning rage and it was hard to turn this into smiles and pretty talk. The rage had to get out somehow, so he vented it upon other members of the crew. He counted them all as his enemies, for they had laughed at him.

20
The Mako Shark

One whose laugh especially stuck in his memory because his cackle was high and shrill was Sails, who looked after the ship's canvas.

Sails had always been a thorn in his flesh. He was older than the captain and sometimes failed to conceal the fact that he had more sense. Having been at sea most of his sixty years he was weather-beaten and wise and did not hesitate to differ with his chief.

A split developed in the mainsail and the captain ordered Sails to patch it up.

'No, no,' said Sails. 'It would only break again.'

'I say patch it up.'

'And I say not,' retorted Sails testily. 'That sail is old and rotten. It's done its duty. I'll chuck it away and put in a new sail.'

'You'll do as I tell you,' thundered Grindle. 'Sail-cloth costs money. We'll have no new sail while the old one can be patched.'

'But it will only bust — '

'If it busts, I'll bust you — so I will by the Holy Harry! I know you, you old fossil. You'll fix it so it will break and then you can say "I told you so".

Well, I'll tell you something. If that sails breaks, you'll take a ride.'

To 'take a ride' was to be tied to the end of a line like a bundle of dirty clothes, heaved overboard and dragged behind the ship.

'You can't scare me,' snapped Sails. But he said no more, for he knew the captain was quite capable of carrying out his threat. Muttering, he set to work on the sail, applying the patch with all the skill of long experience. He didn't want to 'take a ride'. At last he was satisfied that he could do no more. The patch was strong and was stoutly stitched to the canvas; but the canvas itself was thin and brittle.

'It ain't no use,' he said to himself regretfully. 'It will break.'

And so it did. The patched sail had not been up for an hour before a sudden burst of wind split it along the line of the stitching. It broke with a sound like a pistol shot. The captain came running. He found Sails mournfully regarding the whipping rags of canvas.

'I told you it would bust,' he said.

'Yes, you told me,' sneered the captain. 'Then you made sure it would do just what you said. All right, I warned you. I told you what I'd do, and I'll do it. Bruiser! The dragline!'

Angrily Sails turned upon the captain. 'You dare to lay a hand on me and you'll be in irons before the day is over.'

The captain's face burned red. 'You dare to threaten me? You'll feel different about it after you've had a bath. Bruiser!'

Bruiser hesitated. 'He's not as young as he used

to be,' he said. 'I don't know that he could stand it.'

'Who asked you for advice?' stormed the captain. 'Get a bowline on him.'

'It could be murder, sir,' objected Bruiser. 'I want no part of it.'

'Whose murder?' retorted the captain, drawing his gun. 'Perhaps it will be yours if you don't carry out my orders. Now will you tie that line?'

Bruiser looked coolly into the barrel of the captain's revolver. 'No sir, I won't.'

The men had gathered solidly around Bruiser. The captain's angry eyes surveyed them. They said nothing, but he didn't like the way they looked at him. He realized that there was not a man among them who would put a dragline on the old sailmaker.

He seized Sails by the arm and walked him to the aft rail. Deftly he fitted the loop under Sails' shoulders. The proud old sailmaker did not struggle or cry out. The men were coming aft.

'Stop where you are,' commanded the captain. 'I'll shoot the man who takes another step.'

The men stood still, growling, irresolute. Before they could decide what to do the captain stooped, threw his arm round Sails' legs and heaved him over the rail. There was a dull splash as the sailmaker, still silent, dropped into the sea.

Like so many of the older seamen Sails could not swim. His body at once sank out of sight. The line ran out fifty, sixty, seventy feet and then snapped taut on the bitts.

The drag on the line yanked Sails to the surface

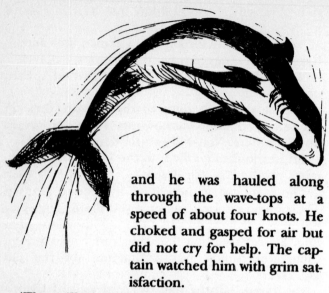

and he was hauled along through the wave-tops at a speed of about four knots. He choked and gasped for air but did not cry for help. The captain watched him with grim satisfaction.

'That will teach the stubborn old fool.'

The men anxiously watched the sea for sharks and killer-whales. There was no sign of the two-foot triangle of a shark's fin, nor the man-high fin of the killer. But just when they began to believe that this part of the sea was free of dangerous fish the surface exploded close to the unfortunate man and up went something blue and white like a fountain, on up twenty feet high, then turned and dived into the sea.

'Mako!' yelled the mate, and the men made a rush to the after rail in defiance of the captain's gun. They seized the line and began to haul it in.

There are sharks and sharks. Many of them are quite harmless. People who have gone in swimming

146

among harmless sharks without being attacked may foolishly believe that all sharks are harmless.

But there are three kinds that are man-eaters. They are the mako, the white shark and the tiger-shark.

The white shark is the largest, reaching a length of forty feet. The tiger-shark is the smallest, about twelve feet long. The mako is the worst and best of the three.

The best because of his blue and white beauty, his amazing speed because he is the swiftest of all fishes, and his spectacular habit of leaping twenty feet into the air (twice as high as the tarpon).

The worst because of his enormous, razor-edged teeth and his utterly savage nature. He is afraid of nothing, always hungry, and always spoiling for a fight.

Twice more the man-eater soared into the sky.

He seemed to be playing with his victim as a cat plays with the mouse that it intends to devour. If he would only continue playing for a few moments the man could be hauled to safety.

The thousand-pound fish went up as if he were as light as a balloon. He was as big and round as a barrel, and as long as three men laid end to end. Each time he came down he dived into the water a little closer to Sails. The sailmaker uttered no

cry and now could not, for the battering waves had shut off his breathing and he was unconscious.

'Pull boys, pull!' yelled Durkins. 'Break your backs!'

A few more pulls and the man would be safe. Now he was actually being lifted out of the water.

But the wily fish knew when to stop playing. Again it leaped, so high that the men had to look up to see it. Gracefully it turned in the air and headed downward. Its great jaws opened. Its huge teeth flashed like ivory in the sun. The jaws closed upon Sails. The line snapped. The shark, with its victim in its teeth, dived deep and was seen no more.

21
Mutiny

The men hauled in the line and looked at the broken end.

Then they turned upon the captain. They were no longer afraid of his gun.

Grindle tried to back away. His face was an ashen grey behind the black bristles. His eyes which usually bulged in anger now bulged with fear. He waved his revolver.

'I'll blast you if you come closer! Get forward, every man of you. It's an order.'

'You'll give no more orders,' said the mate. 'I'm taking your place as master of this ship.'

'That's mutiny,' shouted Grindle.

'It's mutiny,' agreed Durkins, and took another step forward.

'Get back. I'm warning you. I'll report you. I'll have you all hanged.'

'Go ahead and report. And suppose we report what you've just done. Murder, that's what it was.'

'Murder, nothing! Just discipline. He had to be taught a lesson.'

'It was murder. You knew Sails couldn't swim. You knew he was too old for that sort of treatment.

You knew there were sharks about. You threw him out to drown or be killed by sharks. That's the last brute trick you'll ever pull.'

'Mutiny!' again cried Grindle.

'Sure! But any court will say we done right — to arrest a killer. You're under arrest, Grindle.'

The crowd roared its approval.

'Grab him!'

'Clap him in irons!'

'Throw him to the sharks!'

'Tear him apart!'

'Boil him in oil!'

'Give him eighty lashes!'

Every man had some punishment to suggest, each worse than the last.

The captain could not retreat farther; his back was against the rail. Desperately he looked about for a way of escape. His eye caught sight of a vessel on the horizon.

A plan formed swiftly in his mind. He would leap into the sea and pretend to drown. After the *Killer* had gone he would come to the surface. The ship was coming this way. He was a good swimmer and could last out until it picked him up.

But first he must get these hounds back so they would not catch him as he went over the rail.

'Stand back!' he roared. 'I'll count three. If you're not out of the way by that time, I'll fire.'

He counted three. The men kept closing in.

Grindle fired. Bruiser went through the rest of his life with one ear. Grindle fired again. The bullet lodged in the mate's arm. Once more Grindle

151

pulled the trigger. Nothing came from the gun but a futile click.

He hurled the gun with all his might. It caught Jimson a stunning blow on the forehead. Grindle tried to leap the rail, but hands, many hands, were already upon him. He struggled and bit like a wildcat.

Soon he was held so tightly that he could not move a muscle. He could still roar, and roar he did while they dragged him forward and pushed him into the brig.

The door clanged shut and the key turned in the lock. He gripped the bars and looked out between them, raging and roaring like a captured gorilla.

The brig was a miniature jail. Many a ship had a brig, but surely there was no other quite like this one. It looked like a cage intended for a wild animal.

Grindle himself had had it built and had made it as uncomfortable as possible, so that the prisoner would repent of his sins. There were no solid walls, only iron bars all round, and iron bars above. A man could not stand up in it, since it was just four feet high. He must crouch like an animal, or sit.

There was no protection against the weather. The scalding tropical sun beat down upon the inmate during the heat of the day. Cold night winds chilled him and sudden storms soaked every rag on his body.

There was a bunk, but it afforded no rest. The malicious Grindle had ordered that it be made only four feet long. A man could not stretch out on it but must lie humped up in a ball. The men in the fo'c'sle might complain of the boards on which they lay but the prisoner in the brig fared worse. Instead of boards set close together, the bunk was made of slats with three inches between slats. To lie on these slats for an hour was torture, to lie there all night was impossible.

There were no blankets. No food was allowed, except bread and water served once a day.

Grindle had always been extremely proud of his brig. He had enjoyed standing on the outside and looking in at the unlucky prisoner. Now he was on the inside, looking out. For some reason this did not give him as much pleasure.

'I'll have you all hanged, hanged, hanged!' he screamed through the bars. 'See that ship coming? The captain is a friend of mine. He'll come aboard and see what you've done. Mark my words, I'll be out of this thing in an hour. Then I'll have every blasted one of you logged for mutiny.'

Some of the men half believed him. Nervously, they watched the oncoming ship. Grindle saw that he had them scared. He followed up his advantage.

'I'll give you one more chance,' he said. 'Let me out and I'll promise to say nothing about this business. It'll be as if it hadn't happened.'

The men turned to the mate, Durkins, for advice.

'Do you think we ought to turn him loose?' said one. 'I'm not hankerin' to be hanged.'

'Don't let him fool you,' said Durkins. 'He don't know the captain of that ship from Adam. Besides, they ain't comin' to gam with us. See, they've already changed course.'

Sure enough, the motor vessel had turned and was now sailing parallel with the *Killer*, still about three miles off. Durkins studied it through binoculars.

'It's a catcher,' he said.

'What's a catcher?' It was Roger who asked the question, and Mr Scott who answered.

'A ship sent out to catch whales,' he said. 'We do it the old way — they do it the modern way. They kill the whale with a harpoon fired from a cannon. Then they tow it to the factory ship.'

'Factory ship?'

'Yes. You can see it — away beyond — just on the horizon.'

Where sea and sky met Roger could make out not one but a number of ships. One was very large, the others much smaller.

'The small ones are catchers, just like this one,' said Scott. 'The big one is the factory ship.'

'Why do they call it a factory ship?'

'Because it's equipped with all kinds of machinery to turn whales into oil. It takes us all day, sometimes two or three days, to process one whale. A factory ship can put through four dozen whales a day. A large factory ship can keep a fleet of eight or ten catchers busy, combing the seas in search of whales.'

Hal, too, was listening and was as interested as his younger brother.

'It would be great if we could get aboard a factory ship or catcher,' he said, 'and see how the new way compares with the old.'

'Perhaps with good luck, you will,' said Scott.

154

Hal was to remember that remark. 'With good luck,' Scott had said. It was to be bad luck, not good, that would introduce the boys to modern whaling.

22
Escape — Almost

Night closed in over the ship of the mutineers.

The breeze held steady, the sails needed no trimming, the men were idle. Down in the fo'c'sle they ate and talked over the events of the day.

On deck all was quiet. The helmsman dozed over the wheel. The caged captain tried the four-foot bed of slats that he had designed for the discomfort of his men. He gave it up and lay on the deck. The deck was wet with spray, and cold. His dinner had been bread and water.

Grindle was sorry for himself. It did not occur to him to be sorry for all the others he had put into this wretched little prison.

Outside of the brig stood a guard. This was the seaman Brad.

Brad spent half his time watching his prisoner and half regarding the lights of the catcher that had stopped sailing for the night and lay hove to a few miles off.

'Brad,' whispered the captain hoarsely.

Brad came close to the bars.

'Listen,' Grindle whispered. 'How about getting me out of here?'

'Me, get you out? Shut up and go to sleep.'

'It would be worth your while.'

'Why?'

'It would save your neck.'

'I don't know what you're talking about.'

'Heavens, man, don't you know what happens to mutineers? Every man will be hanged by the neck until dead. All except you. If you stick with me I'll see that you get off scot free. Besides, there'll be some cash in it for you. Say two hundred pounds. How does that sound?'

'It sounds crazy,' said Brad. 'Suppose I let you out of there — what would they do to me? They'd slaughter me.'

'They won't have a chance. We'll be off the ship and away before they know what's going on. We'll slip the dory into the water and row over to that catcher.'

'Mmm,' hesitated Brad. 'I dunno. I'll have to think it over.'

'You haven't time to think it over,' urgently whispered Grindle. 'We'll be leaving the catcher astern. You gotta act now, or never. Never mind thinking it over. Just think of your neck.'

Brad felt a noose tightening round his throat. Yes, anything was better than that.

'I'll get the key,' he said.

He slipped aft and down the companion to the supply-room.

At the other end of the ship Roger looked over the edge of his bunk. Hal in the bunk below was fast asleep. The other men had turned in. Only one sputtering, smoking whale-oil lamp had been left burning. Dark shadows crept about the room.

Roger had something on his mind. He would have liked to talk to his brother about it, but didn't want to wake him. Probably everything was all right. But he couldn't help wondering about Brad.

Brad had been posted to guard the brig. Roger had reason to distrust Brad. Brad was the one who had been detailed to hold the lifeline when Roger had spent the night on the dead whale, fighting off the sharks. Brad had gone to sleep on the job. It was no thanks to him that Roger had come out of that night alive. Could such a man be depended upon to guard the brig?

'It's none of my business,' said Roger to himself. The mate had picked Brad and what the mate did was usually right. Roger turned over and tried to go to sleep. He found himself more awake than ever.

'It won't hurt just to take a look.'

He slid down from his bunk, pulled on his trousers and, without bothering to put on his sea-boots, slipped quietly up the companion to the deck.

Hiding behind anything that came handy, the galley, the capstan, the masts, Roger crept close to the brig.

He could make out a black shadow. That must be Brad. He could hear a slight scraping sound as of metal against metal. A key was being slowly turned in the lock.

Then the barred door of the brig was being opened very gradually so that it might not squeak.

Another shadow appeared. That must be the captain.

What should Roger do? He must slip back and rouse the mate.

He left his hiding-place, but before he could gain another he found himself gripped firmly from behind and a great hand clapped over his mouth.

'So, my fine lad,' it was Grindle's hoarse whisper, 'you'd spy on us, would you?'

Brad was already regretting what he had done. 'I told you it wasn't safe. We'll have the whole pack of them on us in a minute. You better get back in the brig.'

'Don't lose your nerve,' retorted the captain. 'As for this young sneak, he won't trouble us long. I'll hold him while you slip your knife into him. A little higher — just over the heart. That will do it.'

Roger felt the prick of the steel point on his bare chest.

'Wait a minute,' said Grindle. 'I have a better idea. He can help row us to the catcher. Keep your knife out. If he hollers, let him have it. Now listen, young fella. I'm going to take my hand off your mouth. If you make a squawk, it'll be your last. Got that clear?'

Roger managed to nod his head.

The hand over his mouth fell away. Grindle pushed him towards the dory. Brad kept close, the point of his knife tickling Roger's back.

'Mind you move quiet,' ordered Grindle. 'And keep outa sight o' the wheel.'

The dory hung from the davits. It was a light cedar craft, half the size of a whale-boat. The two

men and the boy climbed aboard. The falls were released and the boat was eased down slowly and noiselessly to the sea.

The surface was smooth. The wind had dropped and the ship was barely moving. The boat did not slap and bump — all was quiet, and Grindle could congratulate himself on a perfect getaway.

'Cast off!' he whispered.

The boat floated free. Roger stooped to find the oars.

His hand touched the plug.

Each of the ship's boats had a hole in the bottom. It was a round hole about two inches in diameter. It was not meant to let water in, it was there to let water out. The hole was filled by a round wooden plug, like a large cork. When water washed into the boat it was bailed out, but it was impossible to get rid of all of it in this way. So when the boat returned to the ship and was hauled up to the davits the plug was removed from the hole to allow the rest of the water to drain out. Then the plug was replaced.

Roger pretended to be still groping for the oars. His fingers were working to loosen the plug. Finally with a twist and a pull he got it out of the hole and slipped it into his pocket. Then he unshipped his oars and prepared to row.

Water was boiling up into the boat. Roger could already feel it up to his ankles.

'What the Holy Harry!' came Grindle's harsh whisper. 'Where's the water coming from? Those all-fired deck-hands musta forgot to put in the plug. Find it, quick!'

He and Brad searched the boat's bottom for the

missing plug. Roger seized a leather bucket and pretended to bail. The boat was now half full.

Scrambling about between the thwarts the men could not avoid making considerable noise. They bumped into oars and gear. Roger could hear running feet on the ship's deck, then the voice of the helmsman rousing the mate.

The boat was now completely awash. Slowly it rolled over and its occupants were spilled into the sea. They clung to the overturned boat. Grindle obstinately remained silent, but Brad began to yell.

'Help! Help! Help!'

The ship was slowly passing. Soon they would be left behind in the great silent waste of waters. Brad yelled again.

There was a commotion on deck. Men were running, shouting. A whale-boat hit the water.

'Where away?' came a voice.

'Over here,' screamed Brad.

Grindle proudly held his tongue. He held it until he felt a nudging against his leg. A shark? All at once his pride left him and he yelled bloody murder. He kicked and splashed and bellowed. He seemed to go crazy with fear.

Roger watched him with a sly grin. For it was Roger, not a shark, that had nudged him. Again Roger gave him a poke. Again the big bully exploded with terror. Grindle would have been very happy at that moment to be back in his safe little jail.

He began to sob and wail like an oversized baby. His behaviour showed Roger once and for all that a 'tough guy's' bold front may have nothing but jelly behind it. He was seeing Grindle in his true colours — several shades of yellow.

The whale-boat came alongside and the three were hauled aboard. The dory was taken in tow and the whale-boat started back to the ship.

'Who was doing all that blubbering?' asked the mate.

'It was the kid,' said Grindle. 'Scared out of his wits.'

Roger opened his mouth to speak, but decided to say nothing.

Grindle was tempted to make a bigger story out of it.

'We were attacked by sharks,' he said. 'Must have been a dozen of them. I beat them off with my bare fists. Punched them right in the nose. That's a shark's most sensitive point you know — the nose. Lucky for these fellows that they had me along.'

The mate was not fooled. 'Sounds too good to be true,' he said sarcastically.

Back on deck, Grindle was marched to his cage.

'Now you're not going to put me back in there,' complained Grindle. 'Not after me savin' the lives of two men!'

'Not only you,' said the mate, 'but Brad also.' He turned to Roger. 'And I'm afraid we'll have to lock you up too.'

'What for?'

'For desertion. And for helping a prisoner to escape. I never would have thought it of you, kid.'

'Will you let me tell you just what happened?'

'Yes, but you'd better make it good.'

'I saw Brad unlock the brig and let the Captain

out. I started to get you, but they grabbed me. They made me help row the boat. I pulled out the plug so the boat filled with water.'

Grindle laughed. 'The young rascal — he's just trying to save his own skin. Now you'd better let me tell you the truth. The kid was in it with us from the start. He sneaked down and got the key and let me out.'

'Then what did he do with the key?' demanded the mate.

'I don't know — put it in his pocket, I suppose.'

'Search them,' the mate said to Jimson.

Before Jimson could move to do so, Brad was seen to draw something from his pocket and throw it away. He had meant to cast it into the sea, but it struck the rail and bounced back on deck. The mate picked it up. It was the key to the brig.

'Now we have a pretty good idea who unlocked the brig,' the mate said to Roger. 'But that still doesn't prove that you weren't in league with them. How can you prove that you tried to stop them by pulling out the plug?'

'He can't,' snorted Grindle. 'I can tell you all about that plug. I forgot — now I remember. Yesterday I took it out of the boat myself. I put it down in my cabin.'

'Why did you take it out?'

'I had good reason. Some of the men were getting unruly. I suspected some o' them might grab the boat and try to desert. So I hid the plug. Makes sense, don't it?'

'It makes sense,' admitted the mate and turned again to Roger. 'You're in a tough spot, chum. You claim you were loyal to us — that you pulled out the plug so these fellows couldn't get away. The captain says he removed it himself and took it below, then forgot about it. Do we have to search his cabin to find out which of you is telling a straight story?'

'I don't think so,' Roger said. He drew the plug from his trouser pocket and put it in the mate's hand.

Grindle's eyes bulged with surprise. The men cheered. They liked the boy and were happy that he had been able to clear himself. The mate clapped him on the shoulder. 'Good for you, my lad!' he exclaimed. 'You're no lad, you're as good a man as any on this ship. If it hadn't been for you these scum woulda got clean away. Say, we had lemon pie in the officers' mess tonight. Go to the galley and cut yourself a big piece of it. Tell the cook I sent you. And as for you two,' he said to Grindle and Brad, 'since you're so fond of each other's company you'll have plenty of time to enjoy it. Get in there, both of you.' He pushed them into the brig and locked the door.

This time a more reliable man, the big harpooner Jimson, was placed on guard.

23
Can a Whale Sink a Ship?

'Blows! Whale on the lee bow!' shouted the foremast look-out late in the afternoon of the next day.

'Blows! Three points off weather-bow!' came from the look-out on the mainmast.

'Another to leeward!' yelled the first.

'Two straight ahead!' announced the second.

'Whales! A dozen of 'em! Ganging up on us!'

'Whales! Whales! Whales!'

The mate scrambled up the mainmast to the rings. An amazing spectacle lay before him. Ahead and on both sides silver fountains leaped into the sky. At least a dozen whales were sporting in the waves.

They did not behave like the usual school or pod

of whales. This was no family group, quiet and dignified. The height of their spouts showed they were all full-grown monsters, and probably all males.

They flung themselves out of the sea. They soared up like black meteors. They arched above the waves like curved bridges. They threw their enormous tails into the air and brought them down with a gigantic slap.

It was one big wild party.

They seemed to have noticed the ship and were closing in on it — ganging up on it, as the lookout had said.

'Bulls on a rampage!' muttered the mate. 'I only hope they leave us alone.'

Mr Scott on deck was watching the whales through binoculars. Hal and Roger stood beside him.

'What do you make of it?' Hal asked.

'Bachelors out on a binge,' said Scott. 'Whales are like men. Sometimes they leave the ladies and children and go off and raise Cain. The ringleaders may be young bulls that have no families or old bulls who have lost theirs. Sometimes the leaders are ones that have been injured by harpoons or lances, and their suffering makes them wild and dangerous. Usually an old or wounded bull will go off by himself. When they gang up this way it's bad. Just like men. One teddy-boy or hoodlum may lack nerve, but get a dozen of them together and they'll try anything.'

'Why doesn't the mate order the boats lowered?'

'It's too late. The sun has set and it will be dark

in fifteen minutes. It would be risky enough by daylight to run a boat into that pack of rowdies; at night it would be suicide. You'll have to wait until morning.'

'We'll leave them far behind before morning.'

'I doubt it. They're coming closer. They seem to be taking a lot of interest in the ship. Chances are they'll go right along with us. It won't be too pleasant.'

'Why not?' Roger asked. 'I think it will be fun to see them playing around.'

Scott smiled and shook his head. 'They may play rough.'

'But we're safe enough,' said Roger. 'They couldn't do anything to the ship.'

'I hope not,' said Scott doubtfully.

When it was too dark to see more the mate and the look-outs came down from the rings. Mate Durkins and his men stood by the rail, listening.

The whales were now all about the ship. Their spouts whooshed up like rockets.

'Keep out of the way of those spouts,' the mate warned. 'You'll get gassed.'

Hal had already learned this lesson. Most of the men prudently retreated when a whale came too close. One man whose curiosity got the better of him looked down on a whale's head just as the column of gas and steam rose into his face. He was half blinded and went to his bunk with medicated compresses over his eyes.

The whales were a talkative lot. As they dipped, swooped and slid about, they grunted like rhinoceroses, squealed like elephants and bellowed like bulls. Hal remembered the groans of the suffering whale that had carried him so far across the sea. But he had not imagined that the monsters could make so many different sounds.

Evidently they were highly excited. They were having fun with the ship. Perhaps they instinctively knew that they were terrifying the humans on board.

They dived beneath the vessel on one side and came up on the other. One shot up so high that his great box of a head was above the deck. His skull was twice as big as the crate that is used to pack a grand piano. He dropped again into the sea with a thundering splash that sent a shower of spray over the men on deck.

One took to butting the rudder. The wheel was jerked out of the helmsman's hands and went spinning. Luckily the playful beast desisted from this game before completely wrecking the steering-gear of the ship.

There was a crackle and crash up forward.

'There goes the bowsprit,' exclaimed the mate.

He went to investigate. The bowsprit was gone, probably swept away by one flirt of a big bull's tail. The flying jib, the jib and the staysail, previously made fast to the bowsprit, hung in rags.

A monster coming up from beneath lifted the ship a good three feet, then let it drop. The masts shivered and cracked, the sails shook, men sat down hard on the deck, and there was a great clatter in the galley as all the pans on the walls tumbled down on the surprised cook.

'If this is their idea of fun,' said the mate, 'I only hope they don't get serious. Last year a whale gave us a crack that stove in two strakes. Luckily we were near land, but the bark was half full of water before we made port.'

'But a whale can't actually sink a ship, can it?' asked Roger.

'Not only can, but does. There was the *Essex*. She was struck by a big sperm just forward of the fore-chains. It busted her wide open and the pump couldn't save her. The crew had only ten minutes to abandon ship. They got away in three boats. One boat was lost. One got to Chile. One landed on an uninhabited island where the men managed to live on birds' eggs until they were picked up five months later.'

'What an experience!' Hal said.

'Oh, there've been lots of others like it. A whale hit a Peruvian sloop so hard that the men were shaken out of their hammocks and the captain was thrown out of his cabin. Everybody thought the ship had struck a rock. They sounded, but found only deep water. Then the whale came back to finish the job. This time he cracked open the hull just above the kelson and sank the ship.

'And perhaps you've heard of the *Ann Alexander*. A whale they had lanced attacked the ship just abreast the foremast. One whack was enough. The men only had time to tumble into the boats and row clear before the ship went down.'

The mate was rudely interrupted by a whale that thrust its head out of the waves and said 'Rrump!' before sinking back into the sea. Durkins continued.

'Then there was the *Parker Cook*. A mad whale had

to hit it three times before he smashed it. And the *Pocahontas*. Her captain was only twenty-eight, and that's pretty young for a master, so the crew called him the boy-captain. He was pretty smart. After a whale stove in his ship, he kept the pumps going at two hundred and fifty strokes an hour and set out for the nearest port. It was Rio, seven hundred and fifty miles away, but the boy-captain made it.'

'Is it always the sperm that does the damage?' Roger wanted to know.

'Oh no. A finback hulled a hundred-foot craft, the *Dennis Gale*, off Eureka, California. And along the same coast in 1950 a large yacht, the *Lady Linda*, was smashed by a blue whale.'

'I suppose,' Hal said, 'those were all wooden ships. Could a whale do anything to a steel hull?'

'I can tell you something about that,' Scott said. 'Not so long ago a steamer with a steel hull had its plates pushed open by a huge humpback. The break was through the side of the vessel at the coal bunkers. The inrush of water put out the fires and sank the ship in three minutes.'

He paused to smile at the startled look on the boys' faces, then went on.

'You've heard of the great explorer, Roy Chapman Andrews, former director of my museum. He made a study of whales, just as I'm trying to do now. His steamer was nearly sunk by a big sperm, but it lost its enthusiasm when it ran into the propeller and the whirling blades ripped the blubber off its nose.

'Just to give you an idea of the strength of a whale — Dr Andrews tells of the big blue they snagged with a heavy line. That whale dragged the

171

ship forward at six knots, and all the time the engines were at full speed astern! Altogether it towed the steamer thirty miles.

'And he tells of a finback that came at a steamer at high speed and crushed her side like an eggshell. The crew was hardly able to get a small boat over before she went down.

'Of course,' Scott added, 'an ocean liner or a freighter is safe enough. But Dr Andrews reported many cases of whales sinking ships up to three hundred or four hundred tons.'

Hal's eye roamed over the *Killer*. Her tonnage was considerably under three hundred and there was no steel in her sides.

'You'll be scaring the lads,' said Durkins.

'I don't think so,' said Scott. 'They don't scare easily. Anyhow, I think we're in no danger tonight. These rascals are just playing. You haven't hurt them yet. But what do you plan to do tomorrow morning? If you stick one of these rogues with a harpoon I think you are in for trouble.'

'You're probably right,' said Durkins. 'But we'll have to risk that. After all, our business is whaling. There's a lot of oil out there, and we've got to go after it, trouble or no trouble.'

24
The Wreck of the *Killer*

No one on board the whaler slept well that night.

It was an all-night party for the rogue whales. They snorted and squealed like beasts of the jungle. They spouted with a sound like that of a steamer when it blows its stacks, or a steam locomotive when it lets off pressure.

The men in the bunks no sooner began to drift off to sleep than they were roused by the bumping of a mammoth body against the hull or a curious rubbing sound when a monster scraped his back across the keel. Now and then the ship bounced up and down like a wagon going over a rough road. The ship's timbers strained and creaked. Boots on the floor hopped about as if unseen sailors were dancing in them. Whale-oil lamps swung and shivered in their gimbals.

Roger sat up in his bunk with eyes popping when he heard the rush of a whale coming at tremendous speed towards the ship. He waited for the smash of the great head against the timbers.

But the big mischief-maker was just amusing himself. Instead of crashing head-on into the hull, he must have raised his head at the last moment and

struck the rail a glancing blow. There was a crack-
ling, splintering sound as the heavy body smashed
the gunwales. Roger heard Hal in the bunk below
mutter:

'That was a close one.'

Roger lay down again, plugged both ears with his
shirt and tried to sleep.

'All hands on deck!' came the call at dawn.

Usually this call brought a chorus of groans and
mutterings from sleepy sailors. This time there was
none of that. They could hardly wait to get a crack
at their night-time visitors. In two minutes every
man was on deck. The cook dealt out coffee and
hard-tack.

The whales had drawn off about a quarter of a
mile from the ship and were indulging in a sort of
gigantic leapfrog, playfully jumping over each other
in great graceful curves.

'Man the boats!' ordered the mate. 'Lower away!'

The ship had been equipped with four whale-
boats and a dory. One whale-boat had already been
smashed. The other three now put down and pulled
away from the *Killer*'s side.

Hal, in the bow of the mate's boat, was to have
his first experience as a harpooner. Scott with his
cameras was in the second boat, and Roger in the
third. The men all pulled lustily, each crew eager
to get there first.

In the excitement of the chase no one worried
about the danger. This was no ordinary whale-hunt.
They were about to break up a party of gangsters,
the world's biggest. So far the gangsters were only
playful, but what would they do when they felt the

cold iron? But just so long as men, women and children in far cities wanted the things that whales could provide, whalers must take chances.

'We'll make it!' cried the mate. 'Bend your backs. Blister your hands. Three more pulls!'

His boat was the first to break into the circle of monsters. Hugging the steering-oar, he directed the boat alongside the largest bull.

'All right, Hunt! Hop to it.'

Hal dropped the bow-oar, seized the harpoon and stood up. His legs were uncertain under him. His mind was uncertain too. He wanted to succeed in his new task. But he hated to kill. He gritted his teeth, poised the harpoon and waited as the boat slid up to the monster's neck.

'Now!' cried Durkins.

As if in a bad dream, Hal felt his arm fly forward and the harpoon leave his hand. The harpoon went in all the way.

'Couldn't be better,' yelled Durkins. 'Back off!'

As the ship had trembled when butted during the night, so the great whale trembled now. His black hide rippled like water from stem to stern. He seemed to wonder what had struck him. The men waited anxiously. Perhaps he would set off and tow the boat on another 'Nantucket sleigh-ride'. Perhaps he would sound a thousand feet deep and drag the boat after him.

But the big bull did not try to run away. He angled about so that his weak eye could see what had bothered him. Then he came straight for the boat with open jaws.

'Overboard!' shouted the mate.

The men tumbled into the water. The whale took the boat bow on. The mouth from front to back was more than long enough to accommodate a twenty-foot boat. The monster was a good ninety feet, and thirty feet of him was head. Only the sperm among the whales has a head one-third of the length of the body.

So the bow of the boat never tickled his tonsils before he closed his teeth upon its stern. The men who had leaped into the water sank a few feet below its surface, and when they came up again they looked about in amazement.

'Where's the boat?'

There was no sign of it — not even a floating oar.

Then the monster tossed up that mighty head, as big and boxlike as a caravan. He opened his jaws and with a push of his five-ton tongue threw out fragments and splinters of what ten seconds before had been a whale-boat.

Clinging to these scraps, the men anxiously watched the huge black bodies milling about them.

They were used to whales that swim away from danger. These whales did not try to escape. Instead, they seemed about to attack.

They circled around the floating men, snapping their great jaws, thrashing the water into foam with their flukes.

The men looked for the other boats. Surely one of them would come to the rescue.

But they, too, were having trouble. In the third mate's boat the big harpooner Jimson had struck

home. The harpooned whale angrily turned upon his enemies, dived, came up under the boat and tossed it twenty feet into the air.

For a moment the sky was full of flying arms and legs as the men who had been spilled out of the boat fell to the sea. Then the bull savagely smashed the boat with his tail.

He disappeared for a moment, then came rushing back to crunch the floating wood to bits.

The one remaining boat now drew in to pick up the survivors. The big bulls, blowing like thunder, kept circling about, but by great good fortune every man was saved.

With three crews on board the boat was so crowded that any further attempt to capture a whale was out of the question. Loaded to within an inch of the water it laboured slowly back to the ship. The angry whales went along with it. Their beating flukes sent up showers of spray. Again and again they dived beneath the boat and the men held their breath, expecting to be tossed sky high.

What a relief when they were back on deck and the lone whale-boat was swinging from its davits!

The relief did not last long. The whales, instead of taking themselves off, now began to threaten the ship. Boiling with rage they swam round and round, tail-swiped the hull with resounding whacks, scraped beneath the keel.

'Square the yards!' the mate commanded. 'Let's get out of this — fast!'

The sails filled and the ship got under way. For a bark it made good speed, but not good enough.

Its ten knots was insufficient to shake off enemies who could easily go twenty.

Suddenly there was a smashing sound astern. The wheel was usually hard to turn — but now it spun idly in the helmsman's hands. Third mate Brown ran aft to inspect the damage.

'The rudder!' he exclaimed. 'It's gone. One of those brutes has snapped it off.'

Rudderless, the ship fell off course. With her sails slatting, and yards banging against the masts, she slowed to a drift, rocking lazily in the waves.

Now she was a sitting duck at the mercy of the bulls of the sea. It was just a question as to which one would strike the final blow.

A sperm-whale's forehead is straight up and down like a cliff. It is almost as hard and tough as iron. It has been compared to the inside of a horse's hoof, so firm that a lance or harpoon cannot make the slightest dent in it. The eyes and ears are ten feet or more behind the forehead. They cannot be injured if the whale decides to use his head as a battering ram.

So the men went about their work nervously, watching out of the corners of their eyes as a dozen or more of the great black foreheads menaced the ship. The carpenter and some sailors tried to rig a jury-rudder. The mate, well aware of the danger to the vessel, ordered that the whale-boat should be stocked with food and water.

Why was the boat not already stocked? Why were not stores of food and water kept in it at all times, to be ready for any emergency?

For the simple reason that a whale-boat is a boat

to fight whales. It is not intended for storage. There are no lockers or cupboards in it. Boxes and crates of supplies would be seriously in the way, their weight would slow the boat down and they would be lost whenever the boat capsized.

Even at best, a whale-boat is heavily loaded. It must carry not only its crew but oars, mast, sail, harpoons and lances, leather bailing-buckets, wooden tubs for the line and a half mile or more of heavy line.

But now if the whale-boat was to be used not for fighting whales but for escape, the harpoons and lances and tubs of line must be taken out and provisions put in. The men assigned to the job hurried to the supply-room and began to turn up hogsheads of salt pork and tins of hard-tack.

They were interrupted by a cry from the deck followed by a terrific crash and a bursting of timbers. Water thundered into the supply-room and the men in a panic abandoned their work and fled to the deck.

It was the great ninety-foot whale harpooned by Hal that had struck the fatal blow. The men on deck had seen him coming and there was nothing they could do about it. His lashing tail made a wake of foam behind him, and the surf flew up above him like a dozen fountains. His head was half out of water. His speed was terrific. There was no doubt of his intentions. Stung by the pain of the harpoon, he was mad enough to smash his own skull if necessary in order to destroy this floating enemy.

He struck the ship to windward just abaft the

cathead and stove in her starboard bows. Then he floated free, perhaps a little stunned by the blow but otherwise unharmed. His angry left eye was focused upon the ship, and he seemed quite willing and capable of giving it another crack if necessary.

It was not necessary. The ship was sinking. Durkins made a desperate effort to save her.

'Man the pumps! Carpenter — never mind that rudder! Get below. See if you can patch the hole.'

He might as well have cried to the moon for help. The carpenter and his men were not half-way down the companion-way before they were met by a boiling uprush of sea-water which carried them back to the deck.

The pumps had no effect. The ship was settling by the nose. The bow was already under water. Men who hoped to descend into the fo'c'sle to get a few of their belongings found it full from top to bottom.

The water throbbing into the hull made the ship tremble as if terrified by the fate awaiting her and appealing to her crew to save her. And all the time the great bull, with the iron protruding from his neck, lay by and watched, and one could imagine a sardonic grin at the corner of his great mouth.

The masts dipped forward, making their last bow to the relentless sea. The sails shivered as the waves, the fingers of the sea, reached for them. The final dive was now only a matter of moments.

No master, even if he is officially only a second mate, likes to lose his ship. Durkins felt the agony of his vessel, the tremble, the shiver, and it was with the same pain in his own heart that he cried:

'Abandon ship! Into the boats!'

The men made a rush for the whale-boat and the dory. They were filled in an instant, and in another instant were lowered to the sea and cast off.

'Pull away!' ordered Durkins. 'We've got to be well off or we'll be sucked down when she sinks.'

There was a cry from the deck. Who had been left aboard? The captain and Brad in the brig. In the rush of events they had been completely forgotten. They would be drowned like rats in a trap.

'Let them sink!' yelled Bruiser.

'It's what they deserve,' said another.

'We can't leave them without a try,' Durkins said. 'Jimson, you have the key to the brig. Go back and get them.'

'Not me,' said Jimson. 'They ain't worth it. Besides, there's no time. The ship'd go down before I could get them out.'

'And you'd go down with it,' admitted Durkins, 'so I can't order you. Is there a volunteer?'

Silence. It seemed that there was no volunteer. Then Hal spoke up.

'I'll go. Give me the key, Jimson.'

'You're a fool,' said Jimson, and gave him the key.

The boat pulled alongside. The ship was so low in the water that Hal could step from the whale-boat to the deck. He ran to the brig. It looked even more than usual like a cage for wild animals, for the men in it were wild with terror.

'You'd leave us here to drown!' screamed Captain Grindle. 'I'll get you for this.'

The water was already knee-deep on the deck and in the brig. Hal unlocked the door. Without troubling to thank him, the released prisoners ran for the gunwale and tumbled into the boat. Hal followed.

The two boats barely had time to get out of range before the ship with a deep sighing sound, and a trembling and shaking from stem to stern, slid head-first into the sea.

It was a slow dive. Sail after sail disappeared. The foremast was gone. The rings at the head of the mainmast where Roger had stood as look-out sank beneath the surface. The mizenmast struggled for a moment to stay up, but the waves threw their arms about it and pulled it down.

Nothing remained but the stern, standing up like a sore thumb, rudder posts broken where the rudder had been torn away, the name of the ship and its home port visible to the last.

The waves closed in over the painted words, there was a large lazy whirlpool with a pit in its centre from which came a breathing sound, the circling stopped, the surface looked like any other bit of ocean and the sea promptly forgot that there had ever been a bark *Killer* of St Helena.

25
Adrift

The ocean suddenly seemed very large and empty.

The castaways in the two small boats looked in vain for a sail or a plume of smoke. The horizon was bare. There was no sign of the factory ship and its catchers. Even the whales had disappeared.

Some of the men still stared in fascination at the spot where the *Killer* had gone down. It was as if they expected the ship to rise again before their eyes.

The mate counted heads. There were five men in the dory. It was meant for one, or at most two. Only twelve feet long, it was intended merely for use in harbour, by the painter or the carpenter, or a messenger to shore. Now it lay dangerously low and water sloshing into it kept the bailers busy.

Eighteen men filled the whale-boat — it was meant for six. The men stood, shoulder to shoulder. There was no room to unship an oar. They waited, bewildered, doing nothing, knowing nothing they could do.

'At least we can put up the sail,' said the mate.

This was done with difficulty. A line was passed

to the dory, and the whale-boat with the dory in tow began to move sluggishly through the waves.

Captain Grindle was complaining.

'Get off my toes. Quit crowding. Take your elbows out of my ribs. Remember, I'm still master. I'm not going to be jammed in like a common seaman.'

'Stop squawking,' said the mate sharply. 'Don't forget that if Hunt hadn't gone back for you you'd be at the bottom of the sea right now.'

'Small thanks to Hunt,' retorted the captain. 'He did it just to be smart. Just to make himself look big and make me look small. I'm not the man to stand for that. I'll make him suffer for it.'

The mate stared, speechless. How could a man be so ungrateful to the one who had saved his life? Hal Hunt had rescued his worst enemy. The mate was sure he had not done it to be 'smart'. He had done it because it was a job that had to be done. You couldn't stand by and let a man drown, even if that was what he deserved. If Grindle were human, he would appreciate what had been done for him. He wasn't human.

'You're a rat,' said the mate. 'We should have let you go down with the others.'

'Don't be insolent,' snapped Grindle. 'I'm not in the brig now. I'm taking over the command of these boats. I am captain and you will obey my orders.'

Durkins smiled, but did not answer. Grindle's anger rose.

'You think that's funny. I suppose you think it's funny that you lost me my ship. It was your fault. All due to your carelessness and stupidity. I could have saved her.'

'Just how?' asked Durkins.

Grindle evaded the question. 'Never mind that now. Now the thing is to save our skins. I'm the only one who can do that. It's no job for a half-baked second mate. Look at you now — you don't even know where you're going.'

Durkins did not answer. A worried frown creased his forehead. Some of the men looked at him anxiously. Jimson, chief harpooner, ventured to say:

'Mr Durkins sir, begging your pardon, where are we heading?'

'I don't know,' Durkins said honestly. 'I'm just keeping her pointed south. Sooner or later we ought to raise one of the French Islands — perhaps Tahiti, or Bora Bora, or one of the Tuamotus.'

Grindle snorted. 'That shows how little you know about it. The islands are at least five hundred miles away. Loaded the way we are, and what with contrary winds, we'll be lucky if we do ten miles a day. That's fifty days. How can we last fifty days? We haven't a scrap of food or drop of water. In ten days every man in these boats will either be dead or stark staring mad.'

A murmur of agreement ran through the crowd.

'That's right,' said Bruiser. 'The old boy has a point there.'

Durkins realized the uneasy mood of his crew.

'Men,' he said, 'I didn't ask for this job. If you'd rather the Captain would take over, all you got to do is say so. But don't trust his figures. We're closer than five hundred miles to the islands and we might do a lot better than ten a day. Sure, we have no food. But we might snag a few fish, and if it rains we'll catch drinking-water. Some small boats have kept going for six months. We may or may not reach the islands. But we could be picked up tomorrow by a ship. We just have to take our chances. If you think the chances would be better with Grindle, it's up to you. Why don't you vote on it?'

Third mate Brown spoke up.

'The mate has put it to you fair and square,' he said. 'You know what sort of treatment you got from Grindle. If you want to go back to that, vote for him. For Grindle, how many?'

Brad hesitantly raised his hand.

'And for the mate?'

There was a general show of hands, and cheers for the mate. Grindle grumbled and mumbled and cast out dire threats that he would have every last man of the crew hanged until dead.

The hours dragged by. Grindle pushed aside the men who stood close to him and sat down on a thwart. A sitting man took up more room than a man standing, but Grindle had no thought for the comfort of others.

As night came on the men could stand no longer. They slumped down upon the thwarts or in the bottom of the boat, lying across each other, sometimes three deep. In such a case the man in the middle layer was the lucky one, for he was kept warm by the bodies above and below him.

The water that continually splashed into the too heavily loaded boat and the spume from the waves kept everyone wet, and the night wind through wet clothes was chill.

The rising sun was welcome. How good it felt on shivering flesh and cold bones!

But as it rose higher and grew hotter its equatorial fire burned unshaded bodies and parched thirsty throats.

There was no sign of a ship. The only fish that appeared was a hammer-head shark that swam alongside until someone tried to strike it on the nose with an oar. The oar missed its target and the shark swam away.

26
An Albatross Named Bill

Gulls and terns swooped overhead but did not come close enough to be caught. Far above floated a great white albatross.

'I'll bet that's Bill,' said Bruiser. 'He's been following the ship all the way from Hawaii. You'da thought he'da left us when the ship went down, but he's sticking by us. Makes a fella sorta feel better. Good old Bill.'

The greatest of all sea-birds hovered overhead like a sort of blessing. Whalemen have always been fond of the albatross, or 'goney' as they choose to call it.

They are superstitious about it. They imagine the gonies to be the souls of dead sailors, so fond of ships that even after death they choose to follow the vessels day after day across the sea. Antarctic cold does not bother them, nor tropic heat – in fact, three varieties of albatross nest on islands west of Hawaii.

To get closer to living sailors they may perch on the yards, or even on the deck. They have little fear, for they know that sailors will not harm them – dare not, for they might be their own dead comrades. To kill an albatross would bring disaster, as it did to Coleridge's ancient mariner.

The bird the men called Bill had become very tame. He would swoop down behind the ship to pick up scraps. He would come aboard and hang around the galley door waiting for the cook to throw him bits of pork.

He was sometimes in the way when there was work to be done, for he had a wing-spread of twelve feet. But he never stayed long at one time because the motion of the ship made him seasick, and there's nothing more ridiculous or pathetic than a seasick goney.

'He won't stay with us long when he finds we have no food for him,' said Durkins.

Bill lazily circled down until he was just over the whaleboat. He floated, airborne, almost within reach. He held this position without flapping his wings, in fact without the least movement that anyone could see. His great shadow gave the men a little relief from the scorching sun. The men looked up and grinned at the friendly bird. Even when he opened his long hooked bill and gave forth a hoarse 'Br-a-a-a-a!' like the braying of a donkey, Bruiser said:

'Sounds good, don't it?'

'Just like music,' said Jiggs.

And another man put in: 'Sorta like a protectin' angel, ain't he?'

'You sentimental fools!' roared Captain Grindle. 'Slug him with an oar. Pull him down. That's our dinner — pretty stringy meat, but better than nothing.'

191

Some of the men protested loudly. Others were not so sure. Their hunger was greater than their respect for a bird, even if it was the ghost of a dead sailor.

'We'll be ghosts ourselves if we don't eat soon,' grumbled one.

'If he'd take a message for us —' said Roger.

Grindle glared. 'What kind of nonsense is that? In my days boys kept their mouth shut and left the thinking to the men.'

'Wait a minute,' said Scott. 'Perhaps the boy has something there. We have several accounts in the files of our museum of just that sort of thing — I mean, a bird carrying a message. Usually it was an albatross or a frigate-bird — because they love ships — and are large enough to be easily noticed. Since we haven't any food for Bill, he will soon leave us. Chances are he'll make for the nearest ship.'

'But who'll pay any attention to a bird?' objected Grindle.

'We paid attention to this one, didn't we?' said Scott. 'Remember, he's half tame. Likely as not, he'll come down on the spars or the rail, looking for a hand-out. He's so big and handsome and friendly — they'll notice him all right.'

'And how'll he give them our message? He can't talk.'

'Hee-haw! Hee-haw!' said the albatross, sounding more than ever like an indignant donkey. 'Can't talk indeed!' he seemed to be saying. 'Just try me.'

'We won't depend upon his talking. We'll fasten a message to his leg.'

'And who is apt to notice a little wad tied to a bird's leg?' scoffed Grindle.

'We'll tie a ribbon to it.'

Grindle roared with laughter. 'Where do you think you're going to get a ribbon? What do you suppose this is — a girls' school?'

Scott looked down at his shirt. It was a sports shirt, and it happened to be red. 'You fellows get the bird,' he said, 'and I'll supply the ribbon.'

'Still think we ought to eat 'im,' objected Grindle, but he was smothered under the scrambling men reaching for one of the trailing legs of the big bird. The goney kept just beyond their grasp. When one

193

man climbed on another man's shoulders the bird rose a few inches and still floated clear.

Hal Hunt's experience in taking animals alive stood him in good stead now. He made a bight in a line, fashioned a slip-knot, threw the lasso into the air and snared the bird's right foot. The goney was drawn down, braying like a dozen donkeys, pecking at the men with his powerful hooked beak and thrashing his great wings, so strong that they packed the kick of a mule. There were several bruised pates and shoulders before the mightiest

of ocean birds, still braying loudly, was held motionless by many strong hands.

In the meantime Scott had torn a page from
his notebook and with the help of the mate was
constructing a message. He read it to the men:

Crew of the wrecked ship *Killer* adrift in two
boats. Approximate bearings, 150° 5′ West, 3°
South. Sailing South. No food or water. Urgent.

The note was wrapped in a piece of sailcloth cut
from a seaman's coat and tied to the bird's right
leg with a bit of twine frayed from a rope's end.
Scott pulled his shirt out of his slacks and tore from
the bottom edge a long strip two inches wide. The
end of the strip was tied firmly to the bird's leg.

'All right, let him go.'

27
Winged Messenger

The released bird with a final angry squawk soared into the air, the red streamer fluttering behind him. Even at five hundred yards Scott's fiery shirt-tail could be plainly seen.

The goney struck out due west. He seemed delighted to escape from his tormentors.

Nothing could more please the tormentors.

'Disgusted with us, he is,' said Bruiser. 'He's making straight for another ship.' Every hungry and thirsty man had a new spark of courage and hope.

But in an hour the bird was back. He had evidently forgiven his persecutors. Again he hovered over the boat, though he was cautious enough to ride a little higher than before. His red banner fluttered bravely in the breeze.

The men tried to shoo him away. 'Go on — chase yourself!' They made motions of throwing rocks at him, but unfortunately they had no rocks nor anything else to throw. The goney watched with beady eye for any scraps that might be tossed overboard. Afternoon wore into dusk and dusk into night and the bird still floated above.

Again the castaways huddled around and upon each other in the bottom of the boats. Sleep was difficult, due to the nagging misery of hunger and thirst.

But the first man to open his eyes at dawn roused the others with a joyful shout:

'Bill's gone!'

They scanned the sky. There was not a sign of the great white wanderer. Hopes rose high.

'That factory ship we saw can't be more than a few hundred miles away,' Jimson said. 'She had about a dozen catchers. That makes thirteen chances we'll be picked up.'

'Providin' your stupid bird finds the ships,' put in Grindle. 'That goney ain't got radar, you know.'

'Birds have something very much like radar,' said Scott.

Grindle tried another tack. He was determined to turn the men against Durkins. If he could just make a fool of the second mate he might still get back his command.

'If it was me,' he said, 'I'd be makin' straight for Christmas Island. It's due west, and it's a lot closer than your French islands.'

Durkins did not answer. But Bruiser spoke up smartly:

'Shut your trap, Cap. With the wind the way it is we wouldn't get to Christmas by Christmas.'

'Our best bet is south,' said Jimson.

'Our best bet is Bill,' said Scott cheerfully.

But as the fresh morning air gave way to the scorching heat of midday both bets began to seem very poor. The men looked at Durkins with blood-shot eyes, inflamed by sun and brine. Was he doing the right thing? Which would come first, Tahiti or death? And were they idiots to be trusting their lives to a bird?

They splashed sea-water on their clothes. This had a cooling effect, but it did not last. Exposure to sea-water was bringing out salt-water boils.

Hunger was agonizing. Even a belt or a boot began to look good. One man tried chewing a leather bailing-bucket.

A small shark appeared. Jiggs dangled his bare foot over the side to attract it. It was a dangerous experiment, but it would be worth while if he got something to eat.

The shark came closer, eyeing the flashing fish-like thing that trailed through the water. Then it lunged.

Jiggs brought down an oar upon its head, jerking his foot away at the same time.

Perhaps he was fortunate that the shark got only the big toe and not the whole foot. The shark swam away, relishing this titbit, while Jiggs and his companions still went hungry.

Men dying of thirst do not behave like ordinary people. Jiggs felt no pain where the toe had been — he only saw the dripping blood. He caught it in the palm of his hand and drank it. Then Scott bandaged the stump with a fragment of shirt-tail.

Another cold wet night, and another blistering day. Hunger was less, but thirst was more. The stomach had given up its demand for food. But the need for water had become a shrieking pain.

198

Thirst had cracked the lips and swelled the tongue so that every man talked as if he had a baked potato in his mouth. Some began to drink sea-water.

'Better not,' said the mate, 'unless you want to go off your head.'

But the mate thought that he himself must be going out of his mind when at the next dawn he saw a ship on the horizon.

He poked Hal Hunt.

'Do you see what I see? Over yonder.'

Hal rubbed his sore eyes. 'It's a ship and no mistake. A catcher, I think.'

Some of the men cheered faintly. Others were too weak to raise their heads.

'I'll bet she's looking for us,' the mate said.

Grindle peered at the ship. 'She may be looking for us, but she won't find us. We can see her because she's big, but she can't see our sail at this distance.'

'But she's coming straight on. Pretty soon she *will* see us.'

But as they watched the ship veered slowly to the north and then to the north-west. In half an hour she had disappeared.

'I told you so,' said Grindle.

The men sank into a heavy stupor. They lay as they had lain all night, heaped in the bottom of the boat. Even the mate was ready to give up. He closed his eyes and slept.

Hal never knew how much time went by before he heard that whirring sound. Drowsily he looked

up. Then he shouted — as well as anyone could shout with a mouth full of tongue.

'Look!'

Directly over the whale-boat hovered a small helicopter. It settled to within twenty or thirty feet and the pilot looked down. His grin was good to see.

'How goes it?' he shouted.

The mate tried to answer but could not command his voice.

'Got your message by bird,' shouted the pilot. 'Been looking for you for two days. I'll phone the catcher.'

They could hear him speaking over the radio telephone. Then he looked down again.

'Catcher Seven is just over the edge. Perhaps you saw her a while back. She'll be here in half an hour.' And with a friendly wave and another grin he rose to a safe altitude and waited.

The change in the men was remarkable. A few moments before they had been sunk in misery and resigned to death. Now it was as if they had just had a drink of fresh, cold spring-water.

They strained their eyes for a glimpse of the ship. There is was at last, a small white blob that rapidly swelled as the catcher bore down at a speed of fifteen knots.

Hal estimated that she was a vessel of about four hundred tons — a little larger than the bark *Killer*. She had a single smokestack. There were two masts but they bore no sails. Radio antennae stretched between them. At the peak of the forward mast was a crow's nest and in it stood a look-out.

Now the name, Catcher 7, painted on the bows

could be plainly seen. Above it in the very bow was a platform on which stood something that looked like a cannon. Hal knew it must be a harpoon gun.

And to think that there were a dozen of these catchers, every one of them bigger than Captain Grindle's *Killer*. At the masthead of every catcher was a look-out, watching for whales. Even these twelve pairs of eyes were not enough. Also there were the pilots of the little insect-like helicopters which ranged across the sea more swiftly and widely than any catcher could go. Whenever the helicopter pilot sighted a whale he would radio back the news to the nearest catcher.

And all these catchers and copters were just small chickens compared to the great mother hen, the factory ship. A catcher after killing a whale towed it to the factory ship where it was hauled aboard and cut up. The modern floating factory could process more whales in a day than the old-time whale-ship in a month.

After the castaways had been taken aboard the catcher and given a little water and a little food (too much at first would have made them deathly sick) they were made comfortable below deck in the bunks of the crew. There they slept the day out.

At night they received a little more food and water, then slept again while the catcher's crew who had obligingly given up their quarters got through the night as best they could on benches in the messroom.

In the morning there was a bit more to drink and eat, then more sleep. Sleep! It seemed as if they could never get enough of it.

28
Whaling the Easy Way

The first one to bounce back was the youngest. It was about noon when Roger woke to find that his tongue no longer felt like a large potato, the dizziness and dullness were gone from his head, and he was almost tempted to get up.

Presently he heard a running about on the deck above, much shouting, then the boom of a gun. His curiosity got the better of him. He slid out of his bunk, pulled on his clothes and went up on deck. His legs seemed to want to buckle under him, but he managed to make his wobbly way forward.

Several men were moving about on the gun platform. One of them noticed him.

'Come on up, boy,' he called.

Roger climbed the few steps to the platform. The man at the gun greeted him heartily.

'Well, I'll be danged if the kid isn't the first one to get on his feet. Good for you, lad.'

Roger said: 'I thought I heard the gun.'

'So you did, but we missed. A big sperm. He's under now, but he'll probably be up again in a few minutes.'

Roger inspected the gun with interest. It looked quite like a cannon, except that a harpoon projected from its muzzle.

'Know how it works?' asked the gunner.

'Well, I've heard about it,' Roger said. 'There's a bomb in the harpoon. When the harpoon goes into the whale the bomb explodes – and kills the whale.'

'You're ninety per cent right,' grinned the gunner. 'I mean, about ninety per cent of the whalers still use bomb harpoons. We don't. This is the very latest — the *electric* harpoon.'

'How is that better?'

'Several ways. One trouble with the bomb is that when it explodes it scatters bits of steel through the flesh. When the whale goes into the factory these steel fragments damage the saws. Another thing — a bomb killing is very painful. The whale doesn't die at once. He suffers terrible agony. Why make him suffer if it isn't necessary? And there's one more point: agony poisons the meat. Doctors say it's the same way with humans; if you suffer terrible worry or pain your system becomes toxic — poisoned. Toxic whale meat is no good. But with the electric harpoon it's a different story. It packs a wallop of two hundred and twenty volts, one hundred amperes. The electric shock kills the whale before he has time to get poisoned. In ten seconds he's a dead duck. It's as painless as the electric chair.'

Roger smiled. This gunner made the electric chair sound almost attractive. Well, perhaps it was better than a long-drawn-out death agony.

'If the electric harpoon is so good,' he said, 'why don't they all use it?'

'Because it's new. Some of them are afraid it won't work. The most progressive companies already use it – they all will in time. You'll see for yourself what kind of job it does.'

'Breaches!' came a call from the masthead. 'Five points off the weather-bow.'

The whale had surfaced half a mile away. The two-thousand-horsepower diesel of the catcher sprang into action. The catcher raced towards its quarry. The whale was swimming away at full speed, but the catcher swiftly overhauled it.

How easy, Roger thought, compared with the backbreaking labour at the oars of a whale-boat! And how swift. And safe. The monster that could smash a whale-boat to bits and kill its crew was no great danger to the men on the deck of this four-hundred-ton, steel-hulled catcher. Modern methods were certainly more efficient, but they had taken much of the adventure out of whaling.

The catcher slid up beside the speeding whale. The gunner swivelled his gun into position.

'Want to shoot?' he asked Roger. 'When I say "Fire", pull the trigger.'

He sighted the gun carefully, then said: 'Fire!'

Roger pressed the trigger. The harpoon shot out, trailing a line to which was bound an insulated electric wire carrying the fatal charge. The harpoon sank deep just behind the head.

Without a groan, without a tremor, the whale rolled over on its side, dead.

A line was dropped over the tail flukes. With the seventy-ton monster in tow the catcher ploughed on with scarcely any lessening of its former speed.

29
Marvels of the Factory Ship

Late in the afternoon the factory ship hove in sight.
To Roger it looked as big as an aircraft carrier.

'She's a whopper!' he said.

'Thirty thousand tons,' said the gunner who had
befriended him.

Roger thought of the three-hundred-ton *Killer*, a
ship that would have been considered large in the
whaling days of the past century. This vessel was
one hundred times as big.

But not as beautiful. Instead of twenty white sails
billowing in the breeze she carried two grimy
smokestacks. The curious thing about them was
that they were not one behind the other, as on an
ordinary ship, but side by side.

The most amazing thing about this ship was that
it seemed to have lost its rear end. It was chopped
off square. Where the stern should have been was
a great gaping hole, wide enough for two railway
trains.

'They haul the whale right up into the ship

through that hole,' said the gunner. 'You'll see how it works when they take your whale aboard.'

The gunner's words, 'your whale', gave Roger a thrill. Of course, he had only pulled the trigger — yet it was exciting to think that he had shot one of the greatest animals on earth. It was a mixed feeling. Along with the thrill was the regret that the great and wonderful sea monster had had to be killed.

The factory ship was well named. It sounded like a factory. On the *Killer* there had been no sound but the talk of the men. Here the voices of men were drowned by the roar of the machinery.

There was the hum of scores of motors, the rattle of chains, the grinding of gears, the clank of arms of iron that did what human arms had once done. Yet it took men, skilled men, to run the machinery. Roger learned from the gunner that the crew of the factory ship was three hundred strong.

They were close enough now to see half a dozen helicopters perched like ladybirds on the ship's forward deck.

'The others are out looking for whales,' said the gunner. 'We have a dozen altogether.'

The name painted on the bow of the factory ship was *Queen of the South.*

'Why the South?' asked Roger. 'This is the tropics.'

'Yes, but our main business is in the Antarctic. You see, there are international rules that govern whaling. Up here we can take only sperms. Down south, during the season, we can take blues and fin-whales and seis and humpbacks and most any-

thing we like. We're on our way there now. Down there we'll really get busy. We'll be at it day and night. Our factory ship alone processes fifteen hundred whales a year. And this is only one of many. The total catch is over thirty thousand whales a year. Some people think whaling is a thing of the past. On the contrary, it's never been as big as it is today.'

'What kind of a plane is that?' asked Roger, pointing to an indistinct white object floating in the cloud of steam above the factory ship.

'Why, that's your albatross. He's adopted us now. He likes the scraps of blubber that get thrown overboard. We often have an albatross hanging around and wouldn't have paid any attention to this one if it hadn't been for that red rag tied to his foot. We caught him and found your message.'

'Good old Bill!' said Roger fervently.

Catcher 7 snugged up alongside the *Queen of the South*. The twenty-three castaways were taken aboard. Some could walk, others had to be carried, and all were given comfortable quarters in the depths of the great ship. The ship's doctor skilfully attended to their needs.

Roger, still boiling with curiosity, was soon on deck again. There he found Hal and Mr Scott talking to Captain Ramsay of *Queen of the South.*

They were gazing down at the cutting-deck. A whale was being dragged in through the great hole in the ship's stern. A winch groaned as it wound in a steel cable attached to what looked like a gigantic pair of pincers clamped on to the monster's tail.

My whale! thought Roger, but said nothing.

'That was brought in by our catcher,' his big brother informed him.

'You don't say!' said Roger in mock surprise. 'Do tell me all about it.'

Hal was glad to find his younger brother so eager to learn. 'Well, you see, there's a platform in the bow of the catcher, and a gun on the platform.'

'Oh, I see,' said Roger, making his eyes round.

'The gun holds a harpoon instead of a bullet. It fires the harpoon into the whale. There's a bomb in the harpoon — it explodes and kills the whale.'

'Well now, I never!' said Roger. 'Gosh, a kid can learn something new every day if he just has a big brother to tell him things.'

Hal looked at him suspiciously. Just at this moment the gunner of Catcher 7 joined them.

'Well, if it ain't my young friend,' he said. 'That's your whale right there, boy.'

Hal looked puzzled. 'What do you mean — how is it his whale?'

'Why, he shot it, of course.'

Hal stared. 'You young rascal! What were you up to while I was asleep?'

'Oh,' said Roger, 'I was just learning that you can't believe all you hear. Like that about bombs and harpoons. That's old-fashioned. These catchers have electric harpoons. But then — you can't expect to be hep to what's new if you spend all your time sleeping below decks.'

Hal swooped to grab his mischievous brother with every intention of paddling his rear end. But he found himself too weak to move fast and the youngster easily evaded him. The gunner and Captain Ramsay were laughing.

'Yes,' said the captain, 'things change pretty fast nowadays. If you want to see speed, watch the way they put through this whale.'

Roger's whale was already being peeled like a banana. Blubber hooks, operated by machinery, plunged into the hide, took hold and ripped it off in great strips. Knives attacked the strips and cut them into chunks four feet square. More hooks seized the chunks, dragged them to holes in the deck that looked like oversized manholes, and down went the blubber into cookers below deck.

Suddenly there was a shout, a scream from the winches, and the carcass as big as a railway carriage was turned over as easily as one would flip a pancake. Then the other side was peeled in the same way.

Another roar of machinery and the skinned carcass was frisked through a tunnel — Hell's Gate, the captain said it was called because of the rolling steam and deafening noise that came out of it — to the forward deck.

Here there were more machines that sliced off the meat faster than one could carve a turkey. Down went the meat through more holes in the deck. Not just any hole. Each part had a hole of its own, and under each hole was a machine to handle that part of the whale and nothing else.

The liver, weighing a ton, went down to the liver plant. The pituitary gland took a different route, the pancreas another, and so on. Each went down to special pots and special chemists who knew just what to do with them. In five minutes there was nothing left of the whale but the skeleton.

Even that was not to be wasted. Huge power-saws, each fifteen feet long, descended to saw up the great bones and drop the pieces into bone-boilers where the oil would be cooked out of them. What was left would be ground into bonemeal.

It was only half an hour since Roger's whale had come aboard and now it had completely disappeared.

'We can process forty-eight whales in twenty-four hours,' said the captain. 'Thirty minutes for each whale. There are ten thousand tons of machinery on this ship. Most of it you can't see — it's down below. There are two decks under that whale-deck, both of them full of processing plants and laboratories. Also there's a fresh-water plant. The cookers require a lot of water and it must be fresh. We take

213

in salt water and turn it into fresh at the rate of two thousand tons a day. Want to see the bridge?'

They climbed to the bridge. Here there were more wonders. An automatic pilot kept the ship on course. A radar screen showed everything within forty miles. A fathometer told the depth of water beneath the ship. A local phone made it possible to talk to any man anywhere on the vessel. A radio telephone reached far out, so that the captain could chat with the captain of any one of his catchers or the pilot of any one of his helicopters. Not only that — it was just as easy to talk to the owners in London on the other side of the world.

It was even possible to receive messages from whales. When a whale that had been killed could not be brought in at once it was left afloat and a small radio transmitter was shot into its hide. This gave out continuous signals that were picked up by an instrument on the bridge of the factory ship. Thus the location of the floating whale was known exactly and it could be picked up whenever convenient.

The boys were still studying these marvels when another visitor appeared on the bridge. It was Captain Grindle.

'I want to see the captain,' he snapped.

'You're talking to him,' said Captain Ramsay.

'Sir, I am Captain Grindle, master of the bark *Killer.* I have come to demand action. If you don't give it to me at once I'll report you to the police.'

Captain Ramsay gazed with surprise at the bristling Grindle. One of his catchers had saved this man and his crew from almost certain death. He

214

had supposed that Grindle had come up to thank him. Instead of expressing gratitude Grindle was scolding and threatening. At the very least, he was showing very bad manners. However, Captain Ramsay's reply was quiet and polite.

'You have had a very unfortunate experience, Captain Grindle. We are glad to have been of service to you. If there's anything more we can do for you, you have only to let us know.'

'I'll let you know fast enough,' Grindle rasped. 'And if you don't do what I say you'll suffer for it.'

'Now, now, my dear captain,' said Ramsay soothingly. 'I know you've had a rough time of it and it has upset your nerves. Suppose you just relax and tell me what I can do for you.'

'Relax, the man says! Relax!' roared Grindle. 'I'll not relax till this thing is set right. My ship was sunk and we had to take to the boats. You know that much. But I'll bet the skunks didn't tell you the rest of it. They didn't tell you that they mutinied. They didn't tell you that they put me, their captain, in the brig. They didn't tell you that their carelessness sank the ship. They didn't tell you that you have a pack of mutineers on board at this very minute.'

'Well, as a matter of fact,' said Captain Ramsay, 'your second mate has told me the whole story — of course, from his point of view.'

'Then why didn't you clap them in the brig instead of tucking them in soft beds, feeding them pap and having your doctor fussing over them as

215

if they were innocent babes instead of desperate criminals?'

'In the first place,' said Captain Ramsay, 'we have no brig. We don't need it. In the second place, mutiny on your ship is your responsibility, not mine. Of course I'll give you any reasonable assistance. I should say that the first thing for you to do is to notify the owners. Who are they?'

'Kane Whaling Company, St Helena. I'll send Mr Kane a radiogram — and will I make it a sizzler!'

'You can do better than send him a message,' suggested Captain Ramsay. 'You can talk to him.'

'Talk! Do you realize St Helena is half-way round the world from here?'

'Of course.' Captain Ramsay took up the phone and spoke to his radio operator. 'Call the radio station on St Helena. Have them connect with Mr Kane of the Kane Whaling Company. Sunset here — it'll be early morning there. Get him up out of bed if necessary. It's important.'

In an amazingly short time Grindle found himself talking to his boss. True to his word he told a sizzling story. Some of it was true, most of it was not.

He told of the mutiny. He said nothing of the events that had let up to it — the brutalities, the flogging of the men, the harsh treatment of Roger, the death of the sailmaker dragged at the end of a line until he was taken by a shark.

Hal, listening, was astonished to hear his own name mentioned. He was named the chief conspirator. He, Grindle said, had stirred up the men to mutiny, and he should be the first to hang. Grindle, evidently, had never forgiven Hal for telling him he was unfit to command a ship, for beating him in a fight, and, worst of all, for saving him from the sinking ship. Gratitude being an emotion unknown to him, Grindle nursed a grudge because he had had to be rescued by his enemy.

His story told, he listened to Mr Kane's instructions. He nodded and grunted and nodded again, and an evil smile spread over his face. When he put down the phone he seemed highly satisfied.

'My orders are,' he said, 'to place all the mutineers under arrest. Special provision for Hunt — he's to be put in solitary confinement. First chance I get I'm to take 'em all back to Honolulu for a hearing before the British Consul.' He grinned happily and his bristles stood out like black needles. 'They're as good as hanged already.'

'As for arrest,' said Captain Ramsay, 'I can't help you. I can only assure you that they won't escape from this ship. As for transportation, I'll provide it. As soon as your men are able to travel I'll put you all aboard one of my catchers and send you to Honolulu. It's not far — at fifteen knots you should be there in less than two days. You can radio the Honolulu police and have them meet the ship as she docks and jail your mutineers until the time comes for the hearing. I hope you feel that I am giving you every possible co-operation.'

Grindle only grunted. His contemptuous gaze swept over Captain Ramsay and his visitors, and as he stamped his way off the bridge he could be heard mumbling:

'Good as hanged already!'

30
To African Adventure

When the catcher pulled up to the Honolulu docks two days later a row of police-vans were there to meet it.

The mutineers were loaded into the vans and trundled away to enjoy the dubious comforts of the Honolulu jail.

Only two men did not go behind bars — the one who had most to do with the trouble and the one who had least to do with it — Captain Grindle, and his passenger, Mr Scott. Scott took advantage of his freedom to see the British Consul and give him his own honest account of what happened on the *Killer.*

Also he cabled John Hunt at his wild animal farm on Long Island, New York:

'Your boys are in Honolulu jail.'

John Hunt lost no time in winging his way to Honolulu.

At the hearing Grindle told his side of the story and his men told theirs. The result was severely disappointing to Captain Grindle. The Consul in his report to Mr Kane recommended clemency towards the mutineers. The owner cabled back that he would prefer no charges against them.

They were set free.

As for Grindle, who had expected to see his crew hanged, he himself barely escaped the same fate. With all his brutalities exposed to view, he was condemned by press and public all the way from Honolulu to St Helena and back. He was never to command another ship.

John Hunt, famous explorer, collector of wild beasts for zoos and circuses, sat in the garden of the Royal Hawaiian with his two sons and Mr Scott.

They looked out upon the glittering semicircle of Waikiki Beach and the sparkling bay dotted with surf riders, canoes and catamarans. Behind it all rose the grim bulk of Diamond Head.

People strolling by looked at the four curiously. Most of the hotel guests had come from sunless offices on the mainland for a two weeks vacation and looked as pale as if they had lived under stones; but these four were as golden brown as ripe coconuts.

Perhaps some of the passers-by recognized the two boys, for pictures of all the mutineers had appeared in the papers.

Hal said to his father: 'Hope you don't mind being seen with a couple of jailbirds.'

John Hunt smiled.

'No, indeed. Quite the opposite. I'm proud to be seen with you.'

'You have reason to be,' said Scott warmly. 'Your

boys had some tough breaks. When I think of the night Roger put in on that whale fighting off sharks and killers — and the way he prevented Grindle's escape by pulling the plug of the boat — and the way Hal gave Grindle a blubber-bath and later saved him from going down with the ship — I think the boys did you a lot of credit.'

'Anyhow,' said Mr Hunt, 'you certainly packed a lot of experience and adventure into three weeks. It may have been tough, but it's been good education. Perhaps you've had enough of that sort of education for a while and would like to go home and rest.'

The suggestion was not received with enthusiasm. In fact the boys looked as glum as if there had just been a death in the family.

'Who wants to rest?' said Roger. 'We'll have plenty of time to rest when we get to be your age.'

John Hunt laughed. 'And I'm afraid you won't rest then, either. No, the Hunts aren't very good resters. Well, if you don't want to rest, I have another proposition for you.'

The boys perked up immediately. New excitement came into their eyes.

'Whatever it is, we accept,' said Hal.

'Now, don't be in too big a hurry. You may not like it. Africa is quite different from the Pacific.'

'Africa!' exclaimed Roger. His eyes shone like saucers.

'Yes, Africa. Land of the malaria mosquito, the tsetse fly, the crocodile, man-eating lions and leopards and all sorts of uncomfortable things.'

He was trying to scare the boys, but he could see that he was not succeeding.

'Go on,' said Hal. 'What do you want us to do in Africa?'

'Well, we're getting orders for more African animals than we can supply. Some of the zoos want hippos and rhinos and giraffes. A big circus wants elephants and lions. Of course, they all have to be taken alive – and that's a lot harder than taking them dead. I'll go with you and get you started. We can fly from here by way of Hong Kong and Calcutta to Nairobi. We'll engage a good hunter and he'll take us on safari. Think about it until tomorrow morning.'

The boys did not need to think about it — they had already decided. And yet they thought of little else all night. Their dreams were full of roaring lions and rampaging hippos and charging elephants. But they never gave a thought to the most dangerous monsters of the African jungle, the mosquito and the fly.

And how they fared with the creatures of Africa, great and small, will have to be told in another book, *African Adventure*.

Other Adventure Books

The reader is also invited to read *Amazon Adventure*, an account of the experiences of Hal and Roger on an expedition to collect wild animals in the Amazon jungle; *South Sea Adventure*, a story of pearls, a desert island and a raft; *Underwater Adventure*, on the thrills of skin diving in the tropical seas; *Volcano Adventure*, a story of descent into the mountains of fire; *African Adventure*, an exciting tale of the land of big game; *Elephant Adventure*, on a hazardous hunt in the Mountains of the Moon; *Safari Adventure*, on the war against poachers; *Lion Adventure*, on the capture of a man-eater; *Gorilla Adventure*, on the life of the great ape; *Diving Adventure*, set in a city beneath the sea; *Cannibal Adventure*, set in the perilous jungles of New Guinea; *Tiger Adventure*, on a search for rare tigers in the Himalayas; and *Arctic Adventure*, set in the snow-bound wastes of the polar regions.